ACCORDING TO DOYLE

ACCORDING TO DOYLE

Doyle Brunson

Cardoza Publishing

Cardoza Publishing is the foremost gaming publisher in the world, with a library of over 200 up-to-date and easy-to-read books and strategies. These authoritative works are written by the top experts in their fields and with more than 10,000,000 books in print, represent the best-selling and most popular gaming books anywhere.

Visit our web site—www.cardozapub.com—or write for a full list of books and computer strategies.

CARDOZA PUBLISHING
P.O. Box 1500, Cooper Station, New York, NY 10276
Phone (800) 577-WINS
email: cardozapub@aol.com
www.cardozapub.com

From the Author

The recent explosive popularity of poker, along with many emails and phone calls inquiring about this book, have resulted in the republishing of *According to Doyle*. Until its release in 2003 as *Poker Wisdom of a Champion*, this book had been out of print for over twenty years, but the stories in this book remain very vivid to me. I hope every reader not only finds the information within this page useful, but also entertaining. I only wish I could relive every moment you will read about.

—Doyle Brunson

About Doyle

Doyle Brunson, the "Babe Ruth of Poker," is the world's greatest poker player and a legend whose reputation is insurmountable. He is a poker Hall-of-Famer and two-time winner of the World Series of Poker, taking the championship in 1976 and 1977. After winning the series, he co-wrote the poker classic *Doyle Brunson's Super/System* with a hand-picked team of poker superstars. Following the book's success, he put together another book, *According to Doyle*, which was republished as *Poker Wisdom of a Champion* and is now being re-released under its original title. Doyle is also the author of *My 50 Most Memorable Hands* and *Super/System 2,* a sequel to the original *Super/System*. Doyle has made millions of dollars playing poker and has won ten gold bracelets from the World Series of Poker. He continues to play poker almost daily in some of the highest stakes games in the world.

Table of Contents

Introduction

Here is the collected wisdom of Doyle Brunson, the man who has won more money playing poker than anyone else in history. In fact, he has earned over $1,000,000 in public poker tournaments, many of which have been aired on national network television.

In 1976 and 1977, he claimed back-to-back world titles, earning $560,000, a large fortune worth millions today. Most professionals acknowledge that Brunson is the greatest no-limit player ever to walk the earth.

High-stakes poker is a world of remarkable men. Most live by a creed of honor more rigid than anything you'd ever encounter in big business. It's hard to single out one of these players and say you admire him a little more than the rest. Still, I've always felt that way about Doyle Brunson.

Let me tell you something that happened in 1980 that speaks to the extraordinary character of Doyle Brunson. Three years earlier, Doyle had established a business to produce his acclaimed strategy book, *Doyle Brunson's Super/System: A Course in Power Poker.* He'd headed a team of noted collaborators that consisted of world champion Bobby Baldwin, David "Chip" Reese, David Sklansky, Joey Hawthorne and myself. When the project was finished, Doyle dismantled the company and placed an honest young woman in charge of the remaining business.

Left for a year without supervision, something happened. She developed a slot machine habit, continually losing her wages. When her income couldn't sustain her, she began desperately to "borrow" money from Doyle's company while trying to keep the records credible.

You could tell how hurt Doyle was when we found out. I didn't know what to expect. Would he call the police?

I remember that he sat at his desk and took a deep breath as if he were scrutinizing a large pot. Then he looked directly into her eyes. Soft-spoken as always, using his soothing Texas drawl, Doyle said, "I know you didn't mean to do it. Nobody feels worse about this than you do, so I guess it won't do me any good to holler. Sometimes people do things without really knowing why. Deep down, you're still an honest person."

We drove her to the Sahara Hotel in Las Vegas and, because she was broke, Doyle handed her $100. Just before she crossed the street and entered the club, he said, "When you get your head straight, come on back and I'll write you up a recommendation."

Doyle, a former athlete, is very tall and heavy. But it wasn't until then that I truly understood the size of this man.

His advice, much like his character, speaks for itself and is carefully arranged to teach tactics and build bankrolls.

—Mike Caro*

---

*Mike Caro, known as "The Mad Genius," is a leading authority on poker psychology and tactics. He is the author of the acclaimed classic *Caro's Book of Poker Tells*. His expertise and accomplishments have been cited in publications from *Newsweek* to *Playboy* and in over fifty books. In his books, national columns and seminars, he preaches modern scientific poker.

PART I:
Poker for the Wrong Reasons

"A man needs a motive to play poker. For me, it's money."

The Profit Comes from the People

Poker is a game of people. If you remember that, you can bounce your opponents around like tumbleweeds in Texas. If you forget, Lord have mercy on your bankroll.

It was 1961, during the dark ages of poker. There were no world championship tournaments; there was no national press coverage of the poker scene. If you wanted to establish yourself in the poker world of the early sixties, you had to travel what's known as the "Southern Circuit." That means going from game to game throughout Oklahoma, Texas and Arkansas, gathering as many invitations as you can along the way.

I was driving the final fifty miles from Lubbock to Amarillo when my engine started to knock. Pretty soon I was limping along under twenty m.p.h., fully aware of the futility of continuing, but too stubborn to pull over. Now came a terrible clanging, which is how a 1958 Pontiac tells you it wants to be dealt out. I coasted to the roadside.

Well, if you've never had occasion to travel a two-lane county highway through the Texas panhandle, you don't know what it is to be lonely. I mean, you can go for hours and never meet another car. And something else: You've heard about all those cows in Texas? Listen, here I was stranded on a little-traveled highway, worried about missing that night's poker game, and there was not a cow in sight.

Up ahead there was a washed-out billboard that might have been put there in the thirties. It was a spooky feeling. Looking toward Amarillo or back toward Lubbock, it was the same picture—a road as straight as you could imagine, getting thinner and thinner and then vanishing.

I turned on the radio, but all I got was static. Suddenly a car was alongside me, and not just any car. It was a brand new gleaming red Cadillac with a gaudy hood ornament. I found myself staring into the sparkling eyes of a smiling blonde lady in the passenger seat. So taken was I by her charm that it took me a moment to recognize the driver.

He leaned across the woman, shouting at me through the open window. "Whatcha say, Doyle? Need a ride?" His name was Justin, one of the regulars on the circuit. He was a very quiet, unpretentious sort, known for his conservative style of poker: A man who doesn't like to take big chances, and almost never bluffs.

This doesn't figure, I thought. Why is Justin driving a shiny new Cadillac? Why is he wearing a finely tailored western suit with giant monogrammed cufflinks? And who is this glamorous lady beside him? I mean, Justin is the most timid, dollar-conscious poker player you're ever going to meet. Definitely out of character, I told myself.

"Thanks," I said, taking my place in the front seat. "I think I threw a rod."

"You're lucky I happened along. This ain't the main road to Amarillo, you know. Geez, Doyle, why don't you just sell that piece of junk? Get yourself something you can be proud of." He patted the dashboard affectionately.

All this sounded strange, coming from a guy who was driving a '54 Chevy last week. Clearly, this was being said for the woman's benefit. As we sped toward Amarillo, I was pelted by Justin's ideas about how grand and courageous poker players are. He bragged about carrying pocketfuls of money;

and he showed me the lavish diamond ring he bought his new girlfriend.

I was still learning how to play poker in 1961, not yet of championship caliber, but definitely a notch or two above Justin. That's why it came as such a shock to hear Caroline say, "Justin's been telling me how he taught you things about poker. He says you're really talented and you catch on fast."

Justin said, embarrassed, "Umm, well, Doyle always did play pretty good. I just kind of helped him out a little. I bluffed you three times in Lubbock. Bet you didn't know that, did you, Doyle?"

It wasn't true. Justin was just trying to bolster his ego at my expense. But I saw an opportunity here. He wasn't the first player I'd seen lose his bearings due to a woman, or to family problems.

"Ah, Justin, who you tryin' to kid? You can't bluff Doyle Brunson!" I watched him shuffle uncomfortably behind the steering wheel. He had counted on me to go along with his charade.

Now all he could mutter was, "We'll see about that."

I didn't especially want him on my bad side. On the other hand, he was acting mighty ridiculous. He'd never been a close friend, anyhow, and if it came to a choice between humoring him and winning his money . . . Well, you know how it is with gamblers.

So all the way into Amarillo, I refused to play his game. I refused to compliment his play, or testify to the "fact" that he made $5,000 a week—a sum he used impress Caroline.

We arrived at a ranch house that is ten miles north of town. The owner, a typical looking lean Texan, greeted us with, "You boys ready? Game's about to start."

Justin introduced Caroline to the players, and continually flashed a wad of hundreds—about $10,000 all told, much more than he needed for this game. "Let's get down to business, gentlemen," he said boisterously.

Then he glared at me. It wasn't a terribly mean expression; his eyes held the elements of a challenge. So far, so good, I thought. Got better, too.

"Mind if Caroline sits behind me and watches?" Justin inquired. "She's never seen any big-stakes poker before. People are always hearing about guys like us, but never get to see the action." No one objected.

The Rancher walked over and whispered, "It's a damn shame, Doyle. That kid used to be real quiet. Do you know anything about the girl?"

"Not much, except, I think she's going to be expensive."

You can probably guess what happened next. Justin started off trying to turn a medium-limit hold 'em game into a major league contest. Of course, Caroline ate it up, chirping, "My! This is so exciting!" and "I just can't wait to write my little sister!"

For a while this reckless style of play seemed to work, because the other players still thought of Justin as a penny-pincher without a lick of courage. He'd already won fifteen hundred when we collided for the first time. I had a pair of kings in the pocket and after the last card was dealt, he bet $2,300 in an attempt to represent a flush.

I yawned and shoved my chips in almost as fast as he could complete his bet. The swiftness of my call startled him, as was my intention. My thinking was: Since I'm obviously going to make this call anyway, I might as well do everything I can to unravel his temper. If I lose, well, it won't hurt anymore to call fast than to hesitate. If I win, imagine how much more chagrined he'll be if he thinks his bluff is so obvious it isn't worth considering.

"I don't see how you could call," he stormed. "I haven't made a bluff like that in a year!" Then, realizing that his burst of anger was inappropriate, he turned to Caroline. "Well, it was a silly call. A bad break for me. Doyle wouldn't make that call one time in a million!"

I just said, "Hmmm."

Generally, when a man makes a conspicuous bluff and gets caught, he's likely to just sit back and wait for the quality hands, figuring he's sure to get called. But that wisdom should be applied only to opponents whose temperament is stable. At this point, Justin's ego was so wounded you could hear it screaming.

Sure enough, ten minutes later, he came barging into the pot with $2,500 and I snapped him off with a pair of sixes.

"Oh, my goodness," sighed Caroline.

"Shut up!" growled Justin in a most uncharacteristic fashion. Talk about a guy losing his cool! Justin hadn't just lost it; he'd kicked it into orbit.

A few hands later, he shoved his last $500 worth of chips at me with a mixture of daring and hatred. Justin surrendered the last of his bankroll. He grabbed Caroline and stormed out the door like a locomotive without brakes.

I'd like to say I know what happened to Justin, but I don't. Somewhere between Amarillo and Tuesday night's game in Oklahoma City, he got swallowed up.

Yes, poker is a game of people. Things happen in people's lives. Folks change from day to day, minute to minute.

In my book, *Super/System*, I say: "More than any other game, poker depends on understanding your opponent. You've got to know what makes him tick. More importantly, you've got to know what makes him tick at the moment you're involved in a pot with him."

Consider these questions when sizing up an opponent: What's his mood, his feeling? What's his apparent psychological frame of mind right now? Is he in a mood to gamble, or is he just sitting there waiting for the nuts? Is he a loser and on tilt (playing far below his normal capability), or has he screwed down (despite his being a loser) and begun playing his best possible game? Is he a cocky winner who's now playing carelessly and throwing off most of his winnings, or is he a winner who started to play very tight to protect his gains?"

Don't just play your cards, play your people.

 *Proving Who's Best*

This chapter makes three points:

1. It takes patience to teach poker.
2. You can't prove you're a poker wizard in two minutes.
3. Everything that seems obvious was once obscure.

Take Harvey and Helen as an example. Back about 1972, Helen went up to her husband Harvey and said, "Why don't you teach me poker, so I can play tonight. I'm tired of just watching every time we go to a party."

Harvey said, "So why are you telling me now? We've got to get dressed and leave in an hour. There isn't enough time to teach you. You tell her, Doyle."

"Harvey's right. It takes more than an hour to learn poker," I agreed. The game in question was just a sociable one, part of a regular monthly neighborhood party. It was a low-limit, wild-card game held in the basement and neither Harvey nor I ever bothered to play in it.

Helen smiled with pitiful brown eyes at her husband. "Just teach me as much as you can," she pleaded.

So while I watched the last two innings of a baseball game in their living room, Harvey sat Helen down in the dining room and began with, "Now this here is a flush . . ."

About twenty minutes later he was shouting, "No! No! You

don't draw a card. Why would you break a straight to draw to a flush? That's stupid!" Stupid to Harvey, maybe, but not stupid to Helen. She picked up about half the cards and threw them at the ceiling. They danced back down, landing everywhere.

"Why don't you just pick them up, if you're so smart?" she screamed irrationally, storming off toward the bedroom.

"Huh? What did I do?" He turned to me for support.

"You've got to have patience, Harv. When's the first time you figured out you shouldn't break a straight to draw to a flush?"

"What? *When?* I don't know *when!* What kinda question is that? What's the difference when? Are you saying it isn't obvious?"

"Well, how did you feel about it ten seconds *before* it was obvious?" He thought and thought. "That's a good point," he conceded. As I made my exit, he was coaxing his wife out of the bedroom, saying, "I'm sorry . . . I'll teach you right," and meaning it.

Later at the party, Harvey and I walked up to the table to find Helen gleefully stacking up a whole mountain of plastic chips, probably worth five or six dollars, which was a large pot for the game.

She said, "I've got to go to the ladies' room. Wanna play a couple of hands for me, my love?"

"Sure," said Harvey, not realizing what he was getting into. But the second he hit the seat, you could see the apprehension on his face.

Do you know the feeling? You're supposed to be a poker champion and all of your friends at the game know it. They're just beginners. Well, you feel obligated to prove something, right? It's expected of you.

Such was Harvey's plight. One woman joked, "Oh-oh, were in trouble now. We're playing with the professional!"

The game was seven-stud with deuces, fours and tens wild (commonly called Dr. Pepper). Harvey's starting hand was 4-3-6. Without elaborating, let me tell you that this is not a quality hand. He had a wild card with a chance for a straight flush, but even if he made it, it was no sure winner.

There was a double raise by the time the action got to him. He leaned forward and raised again. I know what was going through his mind. Maybe he'd bull his way through the pot, bluffing out these novices. Well, one thing is obvious to me: You can't bluff in a small-stakes seven-stud game with wild cards. But now we're back to talking about what's obvious and what isn't. (How did I feel about it ten seconds before it became obvious, right?)

Naturally, everyone called, leaving him to face five active players for a triple raise. His next card was the seven of spades. This was of no use, since a straight would not win even if he made one. But, again, Harvey got in the last raise.

The final strength of his hand was a 7-high straight, and he was up against four jacks showing (actually two jacks, a 10 and a 4). This was where Harvey tried his last card trick. It was something so sophisticated that his opponent wouldn't be able to handle it.

He checked to the four jacks, muttering, "You might have five jacks, so I better check."

The opponent bet. Harvey raised the limit, crowning the largest pot of the night. Well, the four jacks showing called just as fast as he could sling the chips in. And he didn't have *five* jacks, either.

Helen returned to the game then. Realizing that she had only a few chips left, she cried, "Oh, honey! What happened?"

As we walked back to the game room to play pool, Harvey said, "I figured that guy would pass unless he had another jack or a wild card. I mean, how can he call me when I see that he has four jacks and I'm still raising?"

"Well, brother, if you want my opinion, you *knew* you weren't likely to rake in any chips. You were just desperately trying to impress your friends. Some nights you've got to wait hours to get a decent hand. Poker skill is something that works for you in the long run. You can't let your ego get involved with who gets the best cards on the next deal."

So Harvey just scratched his head and thought for about ten seconds. Then he said, "Yeah, Doyle, that seems obvious to me."

3 Gambling with Girls

A lot of men I know would sooner not gamble against women. I'm one of them, but lately I've had to reshape my thinking. In *Super/System,* I explained how my Texas upbringing made me look on women as too polite for the poker tables. I didn't feel that women should be exposed to the aggression and hard language of high-stakes poker. For that reason, I tended to feel uncomfortable when a woman sat at my table.

Besides, I thought there were only two things that could happen when playing against a woman: you could win and feel guilty or you could lose and feel embarrassed.

Well, maybe I'm mellowing with age, or maybe I'm just weakening in the face of the inevitable. Anyway, over the past few years I've come to accept women more and more on equal terms. One time, I was playing with my partner Jacki Jean in the World Series of Poker mixed doubles event. The way it's set up, you and your partner alternate a half-hour at a time, sharing the same bankroll until one of you gets broke or you win the tournament.

Since there are always four men and four women at a full table, I'd usually be facing four female opponents and only three men. I can't say that those old uncomfortable feelings have evaporated, but after those females threw a couple of unexpected raises at me, I started to play as alertly as possible.

Who says women can't play poker? I've seen women

perform some of the most prudent poker finesses I've ever witnessed. Instead of timidly pushing their chips in, they were betting as aggressively and as wisely as any man. That wasn't my first couple's tournament. In fact, I was lucky enough to win it a few years ago when Starla Thompson was my partner. But this time, the women seemed a lot tougher. Because I've questioned women's ability to play poker in the past, it seems only fair that I commend them at present.

I still remember one of the strangest poker episodes in my life, although I was only ten years old at the time and couldn't really appreciate what was happening.

I was visiting a neighbor. He had an older brother, about eighteen, and a nine-year-old sister. Well, when we walked in, his brother and sister were at the kitchen table where the girl was getting her first poker lesson.

Apparently, the brother took some pride in his poker skills, because he was explaining, "We can't just play for nothing. That ain't poker if you play for free."

"I don't wanna play then," the girl whined.

"Okay, so we won't play. You're the one who wanted to learn."

"Oh, all right. You just wait here." She rushed off to get her allowance, or whatever it was. Anyway, it all added up to fifty-three cents when she put it on the table.

Pretty soon, her brother was screaming, "Why would you call with that hand? That's only a pair of 6s. Are you crazy? I just told you, you need at least two pair to call a bet." Ungraciously, he shoved her the pot.

A few minutes later, he was screaming at her again for drawing to two hearts and two diamonds, catching a diamond and bluffing him out with her all red hand, which she figured was worth something.

"What did you draw to? You drew one card—what did you draw to you little brat?"

"I don't wanna play anymore," the girl pouted.

"You can't quit winners," he pleaded. But she did anyway.

Now I can't say what this proves, but as the girl scraped her coins together and got up, the brother emptied a glass of water on her head. I still remember how she ran off crying for her mother.

4 Pride and Poker

One time, I witnessed one of the silliest plays in the history of poker! My Lord, you can't possibly imagine how bizarre it was. I'm not even sure what you should learn from it, except that pride can cause a man to blow a bundle of money.

The game is deuce-to-seven lowball, also called Kansas City. In this kind of lowball, you can't win with straights or flushes (at least not very often). The very best hand a man can end up with is 7-5-4-3-2 of different suits.

There are three unusual things about this particular game. First, it was at a casino where I'd never seen deuce-to-seven before. Second, it was $20 limit. This game is traditionally played as no-limit. Third, they were using a rule that they tell me has become fairly popular out Gardena way. The rule allows any player to look at his first two cards and then "kill" the pot.

Now, killing a pot is an uncommon practice in the games I'm used to, either in Las Vegas or down in Texas. Although I was just passing through the casino, the novelty of this situation caused me to watch a hand or two. Maybe I'd better tell you what *killing* is all about.

Suppose you're in a limit lowball game where the first person has been forced to open blind. You look at your first two cards and you like them. Under the kill rule, you have the opportunity to put in twice as much as the blind bet, making the limits double what they would normally be.

The way I see it, there are two major disadvantages. First off, it's pretty hard to end up with either a pat hand or a powerful draw even if you *do* like your first two cards. Second, if you snare a mighty hand, players will be reluctant to give you as much action, because they *know* you have at least two potent cards.

But now I'm straying from the point. I watched this scraggly looking, bearded player peek at his first two cards. He hesitated as the next cards came around, and then decided to kill the pot. He slid $40 in front of him. "You looked at three cards!" protested a young man in a blue business suit. "Dealer, he can't kill it. He looked at three!"

But the dealer said that the kill was legal, and that the killer had not peeked at a third card. This judgment was correct; I saw the whole action clearly.

I was standing so that I could see the bearded man's whole hand as he lifted it from the table. It was a 7-6-4-3-2, the second best hand possible in deuce-to-seven! I was thinking, *Oh, Lordy, there's going to be trouble now.*

Sure enough, the man who lodged the original complaint raised. Naturally, you'd expect the killer to reraise, but strangely enough he merely called.

The man in the business suit drew one. I watched in amazement as the killer drew three!

He smirked at his opponent. "Which three cards do you think I looked at, anyway?" His point was clear. Since he was drawing three cards, it would be irrational to assume he'd peeked at another card before killing it. He retained only two cards, obviously the two he looked at when he decided to kill the pot . . . or so an opponent would think.

"I apologize," said the businessman graciously, looking at his new card and then betting.

Incredibly, the killer caught 8-7-5, thought about raising, but then just called.

The bettor came down with an 8-6-5-4-2. "Rough beat. That was a hell of a three-card draw. It deserved a better fate," he sympathized rather insincerely, as he swept in the chips.

By now the bearded player was shaking, obviously mad at himself. He stuffed his remaining chips in his pocket and stormed out of the casino. Like I said, I'm not sure what can be learned from this. But I've always believed that too much pride can get in the way of good poker.

PART II:

A Winning Lifestyle

"Professional Poker is a Way of Life"

 **5** *Never Play Soft*

"You're a rotten sandbagger!" bellowed the Giant, spilling chips as he leaped from his chair. He glared across the table, an expression so fierce that everyone froze and there was absolute silence.

Poor Joey just sat there bewildered and tried to avoid eye contact. Good thing, too. One look into that big man's hateful gaze and he might have fallen dead on the spot.

Now they didn't simply nickname this fellow the "Giant" out of courtesy. He stood 6'7", all muscle, and whenever he walked it was thump-thump-thump and you could feel the floor shake. Right now, it was the man *himself* that was shaking, quivering with the sort of irrational rage you see only once or twice in a lifetime. Big, solid biceps were straining, lips were drawn back and teeth bared, fists were clenching and unclenching.

Joey. How shall I describe Joey? Little. That about sums it up. He was in his thirties, meek and even mannered—a guy everyone seemed to like. He probably had only one enemy in the whole world. But sometimes one's enough.

I guess Joey didn't know what to do. He just sat there studying his poker hand, waiting for the storm to pass and the sun to shine. The Giant paced backward, once and then once again, providing himself with room to circle the table quickly should he decide to attack. His fury increased. He started using the tip of his shoe to make angry sweeping motions on the carpet, beginning in front and ending up behind him.

This unconscious gesture reminded me so much of an enraged bull that it seemed humorous. I almost laughed, but then I thought: *Better not, Doyle. You're the closest one to his size, and if he decides to come after anyone, it could be you.*

Finally the Giant spoke. "You're a sandbagger!" He lowered his voice upon the last word to indicate that it stood for the lowest order of scum. "You sure ain't no gentleman."

"Just playing my cards," Joey murmured.

"Here! That's my hand. Show something better and take the pot." The Giant hurled his cards so that they landed haphazardly face up among the chips in the center of the table. Two queens, two sixes and a 5. The silence was deep and lengthy.

"I said, show your hand!" The Giant was getting impatient. In a voice that had not the trace of a quiver, Joey said, "I raised. What do you do?"

"You *checked*, I bet and then you raised. Where I grew up, that ain't poker! I know you got queens and sixes beat, so show your hand and there won't be any trouble!"

"Do you want to pass or do you want to call?" Well, I just couldn't believe I was hearing right. Joey was acting like a man deliberately trying to get himself killed.

I was thinking: *Oh, Lordy, here it comes! There's going to be a fight, and I'll probably try to be a hero and end up in a hospital. All because of a ridiculous argument over a $20 raise.*

It seemed like five minutes crept by, and you couldn't hear anyone breathing except Joey and the Giant. It was as if the rest of us didn't exist. They were on stage and we were their audience. "Are you going to show your hand or not?" Joey shrugged. "Are you going to call or not?"

It was pretty obvious that the verbal exchange had run its course. If anything was going to happen, it would happen now.

The big man stepped forward, kicked his chair half-heartedly and sat in it.

"Go ahead, Joey. If you want the pot that bad, take it. I think you've got more nerve than brains."

There was a simultaneous exhaling, as if we'd all been holding our breath halfway and hadn't known it.

That should have been the end of it, but as he was raking in the pot, Joey leaned over, flashed me his hand briefly and began to throw it away. The hand was two sevens—a bluff! Why he couldn't have just quietly tossed it into the discards without anyone knowing is beyond me. Sometimes men's egos put them in a lot of jeopardy.

Naturally, the Giant said, "Show it to me, too. Show one player and you gotta show everyone." Sure enough that was the house rule. Joey hesitated, apparently just then realizing the stupidity of his action.

"Show it!" the Giant barked.

So Joey turned over the pair of sevens. "Thank you." That was the only response!

There wasn't a squabble the rest of the night, but then nobody sandbagged, either.

The majority of poker games are played in private homes, and because there aren't any standard rules for poker etiquette, a lot of disputes arise. If you were in a public cardroom where check-raising was allowed, you wouldn't be surprised if someone used the tactic.

A lot of casual Friday night players have written to ask me whether it's ethical to sandbag in a home where everyone is acquainted. The answer is yes. Not just yes, but absolutely yes. It adds to the strategy and makes the game more interesting. Sometimes players will agree to a no-sandbag rule, and then you must abide by it. When that rule is not in effect, and in my opinion it *never* should be, use the check-raise alternative to your best advantage.

Cardoza Publishing 37

The second most debated matter involving poker etiquette is: How hard should you play against your friends? The answer is: As hard as possible. One time, I was walking through a small casino and saw two women pushing, shoving and shouting. The eldest was clearly the aggressor. Out of curiosity, I asked the dealer what had happened. Seems the daughter had bet three aces, causing the mother to throw away a straight. As I was leaving, the older woman was explaining in more normal tones, "You're supposed to have at least a flush to bet against your mother."

I've known a few professionals to enter into soft-play agreements. Usually this means they only bet very strong hands into one another. Problem is, what should other players call with or raise with? Such agreements may begin with good intentions, but they end up being muddled exercises in courtesy. Often, misunderstandings arise and friendships are threatened.

The correct attitude is that folks play poker because the game appeals to them. They like the blend of luck and strategy and are willing to compete for the money. To do this, you need opponents: *real* opponents who are as intent on beating you as you are on destroying them.

By providing good competition, players are celebrating the spirit of poker. Soft play runs contrary to the nature of the game. Those who don't understand the simplicity of that statement should quit playing until they do.

6 Thoughts About Hustling

Lester slapped me on the back and cackled, "If ya can't hustle your friends, who can you hustle?"

I remember feeling betrayed and miserable. I was only fourteen, and Lester was graduating from high school in another month. He had already signed up to join the Navy. He was like an older brother, and he should have had better sense than this.

"Here's a buck and ninety cents," I said, emptying my pockets. "I gotta go home and get you the other ten cents."

Again he slapped me on the back. "Don't bother, Doyle. Just give it to me tomorrow." Then he walked away whistling.

Well, brother, my plans for that day had been blasted away! I'd been eager to walk to the drugstore and play my favorite pinball machine for a few hours. It was only a nickel a game.

Then Lester had come along, flashed a wad of money that must have totaled thirty or forty dollars, and the lure of that big cash just set my head to spinning. You see, we're talking about a lot of pinball games here.

"My old man let me play in his poker game last night. I got real lucky. Heck, you're my friend, Doyle. Tell ya what. We'll try something out. Got any dough on ya?"

"Maybe about two dollars."

"Fine. Well, how'd ya like to win twenty?"

My Lord! You talk about getting a kid's attention! "Swell" was all I could say.

"Well, you're my friend, Doyle. And I think friends should share, don't you? I know you're going to win this bet, because I've tried it with six other kids and I ain't won once!"

Here's where I thought about asking him who those kids were, but he kept rambling on before I could interrupt.

"I just like to play, 'cause it's a guessin' game. You put up your two bucks and if ya win I'll pay twenty. Here's a deck of cards." He handed it to me.

"Shuffle 'em up real good, Doyle." We were standing on his porch. Now I sat on the steps and tried to shuffle the deck in my lap. Finally, I mixed them up enough to satisfy both of us.

Then he explained, "Flip over one card at a time. But first I get to guess if it's red or black. If I don't get at least half of 'em right, I'll give you twenty. But if I get at least twenty-six right out of them fifty-two cards, then you gotta pay me two bucks."

Well, that sounded like mighty good odds to me. So I said "Okay."

"Red," he predicted. Then I turned over the first card, and it was black.

"Hmm, so far I don't have any right. Red again."

Another black card! My pulse began to race, because I had taken an early lead.

"Red." This time it was. Now he had one right out of the first three cards.

"Red." It was black. "Red." Right. "Red." Wrong. Red wrong. Red right. Red right. Red wrong. He had guessed only four out of the first ten correctly.

"Hey, Lester, aren't you ever gonna guess anything but red?"

"Nope." And he didn't. By about the fifteenth card I realized I'd been had. We went through the entire deck and he guessed red every time—and he got twenty-six right. Exactly.

A few days later, he showed me the book where he'd read that little hustle. He slapped me on the back as he often did, but it didn't feel friendly. Our friendship had been tarnished and we drifted apart.

Sure, I felt foolish, and even though I paid the bet in full, including the final ten cents, I never figured it was quite fair.

There are two schools of thought on gambling. One is that a professional gambler should be a hustler. He ought to lie about his ability and scrounge around to find some suckers to fleece.

The other school of thought is that a pro should never hustle. He should seek challenges and earn money because of his reputation as a fair and honorable player. Many gamblers believe they can make more money in the long run without misrepresenting their skills. For instance, weak poker players often challenge world-class pros if they feel comfortable. But once you hustle a man, he no longer feels comfortable. Make a man feel foolish and sooner or later you'll lose his action. I'm proud to belong to this second school of thought. Most of the top pros I know—including Bobby Baldwin, Amarillo Slim and Mike Caro—think the same way about hustling.

I don't want to be so pompous as to dictate how you should run your life, but to me, finding a fair challenge beats searching for suckers.

7 *Broke is Not Fun*

Some pretty sad things happen to poker players.

It's never pleasant to hear about a gambler losing his bankroll. Most professionals I know talk about someone "getting broke." *Getting* broke is different from *going* broke.

Well, maybe it's not actually different, but the meaning just isn't the same. When I say a man "got broke," I mean that it was something that happened to him. People who don't understand gamblers use the term *went broke*, not realizing that it's unkind.

To me, if you say a man went broke, you're implying a failure on his part. You mean that he did something bad, and the fault that he has no money lies squarely on his own shoulders.

Maybe this is picky, and I'm not usually one to quibble over subtleties of the English language. Still, top pros speak of getting broke because they remember the pitfalls and disappointments along the road to the top.

I recall getting broke more times than I can count. At times I'd put my whole bankroll on the table, needing to win just to make expenses and hoping the cards wouldn't be cruel. Sometimes just having the talent isn't enough. Being a favorite is a small consolation when someone's just made an inside straight and raked away your grocery money.

So, let me offer some advice to the world-class gamblers of tomorrow who are still struggling.

One time, I played no-limit hold 'em against a young man named Frank. I knew that someday he was going to be a great player because he already had good knowledge and instincts. Unfortunately, he was going through a phase that's familiar to a lot of us: *Having heart.* That's a term used to describe a competitor whose will to win is all but unstoppable. Typically, a player with heart has $1,000 worth of chips and $100,000 worth of courage. If there's any single fault universal to top-ranking poker pros, it's that they have too much heart! They tend to seek out too-tough competition and risk too much of their bankrolls as proof of their daring.

During my learning years, I fell victim to this trait as much as anyone. I'm relating Frank's story in the hope that it may save you some agony. Although I respected Frank's ability, it was clear that he wasn't playing up to potential. The game was tough, very tough, and he was tossing away too many hands.

In a table crowded with experienced no-limit players, it doesn't take long before those vultures begin zeroing in on a man's weaknesses. One of the biggest differences between limit and no-limit poker is that with no-limit it's usually more expensive to play too tight than too loose.

How can it possibly be worse to play too tight? Isn't most money lost on inferior poker hands? If you're wondering about this, you'd better stay out of no-limit games until you understand the nature of the conflict.

You see, no-limit is a contest of courage. It's much easier to bluff when you can bet any darn thing you feel like. A too-tight player is at a very serious disadvantage because he's seldom willing to call large bets on medium-strength hands.

Back to Frank. Whenever someone would attack him with a sizable bet, he'd fidget in his chair. Usually he'd take a full minute or more before throwing his hand away. It got so ridiculous that I'd just raise him on *anything*, knowing that I was going to win most of the time. Sometimes I'd tease him along, waiting for the appropriate time to make a bet larger than he was willing to call.

His buy-in had been $8,000. About an hour and a half later he was out of chips and he called me away from the table to talk.

He seemed hurt and embarrassed. "I'm really in a bad way, Doyle. Could I get two thousand from you for a few weeks? There are a couple of bills I need to take care of."

Knowing him to be honorable, I granted his request. He said, "It seems you just never win when you *need* the money"

And that's exactly the point. I've met maybe ten men in my life that can play excellent poker under extreme pressure. When the rent money's on the table, it's hard to make tough calls that might put you out of action.

I think it's better to wind down and play a smaller game, a game you can afford. Right next to the big game where Frank got broke was a medium-limit hold 'em contest where he could have won or lost no more than $2,000.

Sure, it's hard to knock down the size of your gambling, especially after you've suffered several bad losses in a row. You're tempted to try to get it all back at once. Most truly successful poker players have learned to do otherwise. After a bad run, they're willing to play smaller, committing weeks or even months to the recovery.

I suppose this is the best advice I can give: When you're down near the bottom of your bankroll, never play in a game where you feel uncomfortable. Also, stay away from no-limit.

Sadly, I've violated that advice a hundred times in my life. It's the nature of a gambler to want to take chances. Yes, I still remember what it feels like to "get broke."

8 *Honor in Gambling*

"Never trust a gambler."

Maybe you've heard those words before, because they echo through the minds and they spill from the mouths of Middle America. Whenever I hear someone say that, it's like a spark to my temper. I don't rightly know how gamblers gained the reputation as untrustworthy, disreputable scoundrels. But in many folks' minds, that's what a gambler is.

In truth, a professional gambler is among the most honorable of men. I've known a man to walk through four miles of blizzard after his car stalled just to pay a debt on time. I've seen gamblers go hungry to honor a bet even though no pressure was placed on them.

I shy away from legal contracts. If I can't trust a man's word, then I don't want to do business with him.

A few years back, I was marketing *Super/System*, and a man came to my office explaining how he could arrange interviews on all the TV networks and triple my book sales.

We talked for a while, and the man seemed qualified. So I said, "Go ahead, see what you can do."

He seemed startled at this and gasped, "Wh-what do you mean?"

"I mean I'm impressed, and if you can get something going, I'll treat you fairly."

There was a long pause. "Well, there's a little matter of a contract," he said.

"Why?"

"Because I don't want to work day and night and put this thing together and then have you say we didn't have a deal. Not that you'd say that or anything, but some people . . ."

I told him, "You've got a deal if you want it. If my handshake's good enough for you, then your word's good enough for me."

"Well, it's not that I don't trust you, Doyle, but I've been burned so many times by people not doing what they say they're going to do. And you *are* a gambler. Nothing wrong with that, mind you, but . . ."

"If you change your mind, let me know," I said, and I escorted him from my office. He never came back.

You'd be surprised how many deals gamblers make on the strength of a handshake. Every day I read about some businessman or another tied up in court over some disagreement. Everyone is trying to get the best of someone else.

Gamblers don't think that way. That's why you can shout a $10,000 bet at a gambler clear across a poker room and know you're going to get paid the same day if you win it.

This reminds me of the silliest episode I ever did see involving gamblers and trust. This young kid, Bradley, came to Fort Worth to play cards. He attended the game regularly for a few days, playing really scared poker. Then he noticed that there was a lot of sports action going on; a lot of players were betting on football.

Well, he wanted to make a $1,000 bet on Denver (back when the Broncos were still in the American Football League). I liked the other side, so I took the kid's bet.

"Okay, could you write out a receipt?" Bradley asked.

At this, all the regular players broke out in spontaneous laughter that didn't stop.

"You mean you want a receipt for a football bet?" I couldn't stop laughing either.

"Well, just in case you forget. It's a lot of money for me, so I want to make sure."

Normally, I would have refused, but it seemed so silly that I just had to do it. It wasn't a receipt for money, just a note saying who he bet on and how much.

It was Sunday and we were watching another game, but the score of the Denver game was flashing on the screen from time to time. Denver was winning big. In the meantime, Bradley laid his "receipt" next to his ashtray and, as a practical joke, a friend of mine touched his cigarette to it.

Just at the perfect moment, while the receipt was turning to crispy ashes, the final Denver score was given. Denver won.

Unaware of the small fire, Bradley jumped from his chair and cried gleefully.

I said, "Give me your receipt and I'll pay you right now."

So Bradley reached for his receipt and there was just a black twisted remnant.

He was plenty scared. "You guys are all witnesses," he said. "You all know what the bet was."

Everyone just grumbled and said that they didn't want to get involved. After whimpering and pacing the floor for about ten minutes, Bradley suggested, "Pay me half of it, Doyle? I'll settle for half."

"Do you trust me, Bradley?"

"Of course I trust you, Doyle. If I didn't trust you, I wouldn't bet in the first place. I really trust you a lot." He was very nervous now.

I handed him the full $1,000, of course. It was simply a matter of honor. In my mind there has never been a law, a receipt or a legal document ever written that is worth half as much as a gambler's word.

9   *Are You Ready to Win*

Not long ago a newspaper reporter asked, "When you play poker, is there any way you can tell in advance if you're going to win?" I remember saying, "Not really. That's part of the suspense. Sometimes the cards fall the way you like and sometimes they bring rude surprises." That quote seemed to appeal to her, because she jotted it down with a smile.

But, you know, as I was driving home that night after a sizable and satisfying win, I remembered how exceptionally confident I'd felt before playing. I thought back over all the other times I'd felt really optimistic beforehand. Almost all had turned out profitably. Then I thought back over the occasions when I'd felt hesitant about playing. I recalled those secret mental messages that had warned me I was in for a long night. More often than not, those warnings were dead on target.

It's easy to give credit to your psychic powers, but I think the truth is a lot less mysterious. The more I thought about it, the clearer it was that there were real reasons why I should have felt confident before winning. Likewise, there were valid explanations for my feelings of uncertainty before losing.

In football, coaches and trainers examine their athletes carefully before each contest. They demand good information about their team's mental and physical condition. Not many poker players examine themselves before a game. Most merely barge in, not giving the slightest thought to their preparedness.

Poker players think that one night is pretty much like the next. If you searched their souls, they'd swear that they could play nearly as well tired or sick as they could any other time. That's a serious mistake. Players would do well to examine themselves carefully before every poker game. Occasionally they should place themselves on an injury list and declare themselves ineligible.

Brother, what I think happens is that even when you consciously ignore the warning signals, your subconscious mind keeps screaming that all is not right. When you play in spite of this, you're likely to lose.

I've developed a short checklist for deciding whether or not to play:

1. Have you had enough sleep? If no, don't play.
2. Is there something else you'd rather be doing? If yes, don't play.
3. Are you feeling physically well enough to sit through a movie? If no, don't play. When you have a headache or you'd be tired or fidgety in a theater, you probably won't play your best poker.
4. Are you so mad at someone that it's interfering with your concentration? If yes, don't play.
5. Are drugs, alcohol, or medication interfering with your logical thinking? If yes, don't play.
6. Are you emotionally upset? If yes, don't play. Fights with your wife or girlfriend are not healthy to your money clip. And most important:
7. Do you feel you're going to win? If no, don't play. Give credibility to your hidden feelings. Your subconscious mind might be analyzing things you're not aware of.

If it looks like a good game and you survive the checklist, then sit down and do some serious winning. Otherwise, save your energy for tomorrow.

10 World Class Intimidation

"I'm a pretty tough poker player, myself," bragged the plumber as he fixed my kitchen faucet.

He banged on his wrench a couple of times, swore, "This devil's really on there tight," and gave it a particularly brisk slap with an open palm.

Whatever he was attacking seemed to yield and he scooted out from beneath the sink smiling faintly. "Yeah, Doyle, you an' me oughta sit down sometime and discuss poker. Bet we'd both enjoy it."

"Umm," I said.

"I read just about everything they ever wrote on it," he explained. "Got me your book, plus some stuff by Scarne and a lot of others. Problem is, you guys don't go far enough. I knew that stuff since I was a kid." He looked to be about twenty-three, and that's still a kid to me.

Feeling trapped, and wanting to give this guy no provocation to sabotage my kitchen sink, I talked cordially for a few minutes. "I agree with what you said in the book—you should never play a hold 'em hand with a queen in it."

Well, brother, that wasn't in the book! Neither was any of the other poker "knowledge" he threw at me. He seemed like a nice enough fellow, but after about five minutes, I excused myself and thanked him for the fine job he was doing.

Pointless story? Nope. It seems to me that many players

who buy poker literature read it mighty haphazardly. That, in itself, isn't too damaging, but it means they receive far from maximum value for their purchases. The problem, as I see it, is this: Just the fact that a new book is in their possession gives some players the incentive to take daring strides into games they have no business playing.

Maybe they feel there's some sort of magic that comes with mere ownership of the book. You see them sit smugly at tables, unarmed but eager for battle. Their subsequent doom is always self-inflicted. Yes, a lot of good stuff has been written about poker recently, and more is coming out all the time. But you've got to *read* it to learn anything. Just brushing across the words absent-mindedly while watching television won't do the trick. But a lot of folks think that will do the trick, and there's the problem.

A book cannot reward you unless you read it. Well, if that seems obvious, here's another bit of advice that ought to be obvious. In hold 'em you should always be conscious of the best possible hand your opponent can have at any given time. Is that too simple to merit mention?

You'd be surprised how many average poker players don't know at any moment what the best hand is that an opponent might have. Here's an episode described in 1978 world champion Bobby Baldwin's book, *Winning Poker Secrets.* It really happened, and it's a pretty powerful example of both these things that I'm talking about.

If you don't understand the mechanics of hold 'em, it's played like this: Each player is dealt two cards. There is a round of betting. Then three cards are dealt face up. These are called the "flop" and are shared equally by all players so that the strength of a hand consists of the two cards held privately by each player in combination with the three face-up communal cards. There is another round of betting, another card is dealt up, another betting round, a final up card, and then the last round of betting.

In all, each player holds two cards known only to him and five face-up cards shared with his opponents. It is the best five-card combination out of seven cards that comprises a player's hand.

The following story happened just before the 1978 World Series of Poker at Binion's Horseshoe Casino. It's taken from Baldwin's book, with his permission:

> We got to socializing in the coffee shop. Turned out his name was Chet Tower and he owned forty-seven laundromats and a couple of restaurants. Two hours later we were at a table consisting of me, Puggy Pearson, Doyle and two other professionals.
>
> Chet was so glad to meet Doyle that I thought the game would never get started. He just laid it on real thick about how he'd enjoyed the hold 'em sections in the book. He said he'd just got his $100 copy yesterday and had already digested it. Naturally, Doyle and I were a bit skeptical. We started playing, and it became clear that Chet had not mastered as much of the game as he thought.
>
> Finally I got involved in a large pot with this neophyte gambler. He brought it in for $800 and I called with just a 5 and a 3. It was the sort of hand I liked to stay for the flop with whenever he let me in cheaply.
>
> The flop was K-9-2. I checked, preparing to give up the hand now that nothing helpful had flopped. He checked also. The next card was a 6. Except for the remote possibility of making an inside straight, my hand was hopeless. So I checked, again ready to fold should he make an even smaller wager. Again he checked. So we got the last card. The dealer turned it up slowly. It was a 4.
>
> "Well, now," I thought, "this makes the picture a little different." Suddenly I had a straight. More than that, I

was holding the best possible hand. I started debating how much to bet, but then I noticed the way his hand was unconsciously inching toward his stack. He was going to bet. I was positive!

"Check to you, Chet."

He didn't even hesitate. "I'll make a small wager. Say . . . oh . . . say about fifteen hundred." He pushed his bet neatly into the pot. I figured, if ever a man looked ready to call a disproportionately large bet, it was Chet Tower. I raised him $36,000.

He literally turned white. I've never seen anything like it. I was afraid he might be having a heart attack. His breathing was very labored. Well, he thought and thought. And thought. Then he slumped back to his chair in virtual resignation. For a moment I thought I'd lost the call. Finally he said, "Bobby, I guess you've got me. But I can't see how I can throw this hand away..." He started counting through his chips. When he finished, he slid them into the pot, calling my bet and leaving him only about $12,000 in front of him.

He turned his hand over at the same time I did. 5-3! Well, I tell you, I've never played a weirder hand. I mean, the guy had the absolute nuts. We both did. There was no possible way either of us could lose. But he had almost folded, and finally, reluctantly, he'd called without even raising his last $12,000.

That story illustrates two things:

1. Players who think that the mere ownership of a poker book will improve their chances are apt to barge headlong into a heap of trouble.
2. The first thing you should consider in hold 'em is the best possible hand your opponent can hold.

But this story really underscores a third point as well: All of the world's top pros practice an aggressive style that I call *Power Poker.* The fact that Chet failed to raise with the perfect hand shows how thoroughly intimidating this strategy can be.

PART III:

Bad Habits

"There's almost no limit to how much you can win playing good poker. About the only thing you can't afford is a bad habit."

11 Marathon Madness

Bingo winked at me. It was 1968; he was a young poker pro in top form. This morning he was really moving in for the kill, and he knew it.

There were four players gathered around a cigarette-burned table at a cafe in Waco, Texas. All four were superior players, darn near as good as Bingo himself. There was only one problem with them this fine spring morning: The sun was rising merrily and this was the third morning they'd seen that happen without hitting the pillow.

You talk about a scraggly group of players! Tom was napping between hands; Eddie was frowning from lack of sleep; Bill and his brother Bob looked like ghosts with glassy eyes that could scarcely stay open. Well, sir, you might occasionally see a game this deteriorated in someone's basement in Denver—you know, just some good ol' boys on a lost weekend that started with a Friday night game that missed its midnight deadline.

Only one difference here: These guys weren't playing quarter-limit. There was $40,000 worth of chips and over $20,000 cash on the table. Sixty grand, and these guys didn't even know what day it was!

In the background, Bob (the older brother, though no man at the table was more than twenty-eight) was mumbling, "Whose deal is it, darn it! Didn't I deal last time? No, you dealt. No, I did deal. Oh, what's the difference?"

It was into this strawberry patch of a poker game that tall, lanky and ever-so-cocky Bingo strode. He was just about as fresh as a new billboard rising from the Texas panhandle. His hair was still damp from a recent shower and he even wore a flower in his lapel—something we'd all learned to tolerate about him, although it seemed a mite out of place down in Waco.

"Leaving, Doyle?" he chirped.

"Yeah, Bingo, I've just about had it," I admitted. I was a $5,000 winner and about two days, dead tired. Although I've played longer, this was about my limit. Sure, I could force it a little more, but that would become pure misery. One other thing, I sure didn't want to compete against someone fresh. My history was that in a table full of weary poker warriors, the guy with eight hours sleep, a shower and a hearty breakfast just about always got the money.

So, Bingo sat down to feast on the situation. But when I returned ten hours later, he had hit an incredibly bad run and was a $30,000 loser.

Meanwhile, Tom and Eddie had taken six-hour naps on nearby sofas while the brothers sleepily held Bingo off. They just hit miracle after miracle, Bingo later complained to me.

Then Bob and Bill hit the sofas while the rejuvenated Tom and Eddie began to demolish Bingo. Two days later I came in to play. The game was eight-handed and I had to line up for a seat. Everyone was fresh or at least halfway fresh, except Bingo, of course. He was bearded and dismantled—a sorry-looking Easterner if ever there was one.

Down fifty grand, Bingo turned around and looked at me dismally, scarcely aware of my presence. "What should I do, Doyle?" he asked almost tearfully, a dim twinge of rationality gleaming in his eyes. "I just reckon you oughta quit, Bingo," I advised.

And so he did, brother. So he did.

12 Human Kindness

There's a small ranch near Dallas where I used to play in the late '60s. The game was mostly pot-limit hold 'em, which was unusual because most of my playing experience was no-limit.

They'll try to tell you there's very little difference between pot-limit and no-limit. They say pot-size bets are the norm in no-limit anyway. Well, maybe some no-limit players may find those two poker types harmonious, but my style of play puts me at a severe handicap in pot-limit. That's because I like to move all-in from time to time. Sometimes, I'll slide a mountain of chips into the pot, chasing just a few dollars. Once in a while, I'll do it with a bluffing hand.

Wouldn't a smaller bet make more sense? Not if an extra-large bet confuses your opponent. More than that, now and then you'll stumble on a player who never finds the courage to call a painfully large bet. One more thing: When a man is facing a bet awesome enough to make him worry, he doesn't always think clearly. He's apt to make a bad decision, and that's mighty expensive for him and mighty profitable for you.

Yes sir, I'll take no-limit over pot-limit any day! But that's not really the point of this chapter. There was this guy Elmer who also preferred no-limit. He was fifty years old the first day he sat down at the ranch house. I mean, he was exactly fifty years old that day, because he made a big point of it. We all wished him happy birthday.

But, at first, there was no present that accompanied our good wishes; in fact, we just gobbled him up real fast. To begin with, he bought in for $1,000. It disappeared after the second hand.

He grumbled, "I never was much for pot-limit. It's like putting a forty mile an hour limit on Route 66." He bought himself another two grand.

He had a lot of confidence; I'll say that for Elmer. And his correct posture and winning attitude didn't crumble, even after that $2,000 was lost. This time he bought in for $4,000. But when that evaporated, you could see his composure fall apart.

"Might as well make it an even ten thousand," he sighed, counting out thirty hundreds and taking the chips from the host.

Although this was a moderately big game with two blinds of $5 and $10, Elmer was nearing the unofficial house record for biggest loss. I guess we all felt a little sorry for him, because he wasn't playing bad poker. Bad fortune seemed to hover over his head with every turn of the card. But at the same time I felt sympathy, I remembered all the really bad streaks I'd personally suffered, and somehow took an unhealthy delight in the fact that this was happening to someone *else*. And although, intellectually, I felt no joy in Elmer's misfortune, I certainly wasn't going to let him off the hook if I could help it.

He staged a short and insignificant comeback, and then, about three hours deep into the game, I made a straight down the river and shot down his three queens. The last of his composure evaporated so quickly you could almost see it being sucked out of him. After that hand, he had only $900 left. Within five minutes that had dwindled to $10.

It was his big blind, so he pushed his last two chips onto the table in front of him. Seven players passed quickly. Then the small blind had to act. A skinny Oklahoman named Paul looked at his cards and then at Elmer, and then back at his cards again.

Finally he said, "I'll tell you what, Elmer. I'm going to let you have this pot. Maybe it'll change your luck. Happy birthday." He flipped two aces face-up on the table for everyone to see what a gentleman he was.

Elmer muttered the expected "thank you" and promptly doubled his money on the next pot. Well, that got things rolling for him. For the next four hours, he terrorized the table. Things really sizzled for him. Everyone got hurt a little, but mostly he kept pounding on Paul. Finally Elmer had $14,000 worth of chips and Paul got flat broke.

Now Paul tried to get a check cashed, but there was a strict house rule against it. So he turned to Elmer and reminded him, "Looks like I did you some good when I didn't take your last ten bucks with a pair of aces."

"Looks like you did," Elmer agreed.

Paul waited for some additional words, but Elmer held silent. "Well, look," Paul pleaded, "how 'bout you lending me a thousand."

"Sorry, I can't do that," Elmer explained. "I don't believe you should help a man out in a poker game. Heck, you'd probably just turn around and beat me. I don't mean to be rude, and I appreciate your kindness, but I just can't help you."

There's a lesson to be learned here. It's fine to *feel* sympathetic toward an opponent, but when you act sympathetic at the table, that isn't poker. Eventually Elmer loaned Paul $20 pocket money to take home. I suppose it was an act of human kindness.

13 A Sad Tale of Superstition

Just about anyone will tell you that gamblers are superstitious. They wear lucky shirts, hats, socks and shoes. Often good-luck charms hang from their necks. They can look pretty ridiculous changing seats and avoiding evil numbers.

"It isn't easy finding your lucky numbers, Doyle," complained a woman who comes to Las Vegas one week a year to play roulette. "I mean, just when you think you've got the numbers figured out, they change on you."

Talk like that may seem just plain silly to the professional gambler who has faith in the odds and does not allow superstition to control his life. Still, I suspect that many of my fellow poker pros do things now and again just for purely superstitious reasons. They won't admit it, of course, but they do it.

The tragic part of all this is that many a man, who could otherwise have succeeded in the tough pro-poker arena, has fallen victim to the superstition game. I recall one promising young player from Ohio who refused to begin with a pair of aces or kings in hold 'em because he had a real powerful dream that he'd immediately go broke. He got broke anyway, but that was because he never played his kings and aces.

Probably the weirdest superstition of all belonged to this guy Alexander from Canada. When he first started playing regular at the Dunes, we all tried calling him Alex. Seemed that was the natural thing. But he always got hot and said, "The name's Alexander!" Then he'd spell it for us.

Once, after someone had called him Alex, he stood up in the middle of a poker table and screamed, "Alexander! Alexander! Alexander!" He must have shouted his name twenty times before he calmed down and took his seat. So, what would you do? We called him Alexander, like he wanted.

He wasn't a good player, and no one expected him to leave town with any money. But he brought quite a bankroll—over $200,000 we decided, thinking back over it. He was now in his third week, and still surviving.

I'll never forget his last night. He came to the table wearing the strangest shirt a man could imagine. It had pockets everywhere: little pockets, giant pockets, pockets made out of felt and pockets made out of paper! We knew better than to comment, fearing he'd go into one of his typical tirades.

The game was no-limit hold 'em. He sat next to me and said, "Deal me out. I just want to watch a few hands."

So I played a hand and won it with four sixes—the two on the board matching the two I held in my hand. Rip!

I turned, startled. Alexander had torn one of his pockets! We all were curious about his motive, of course, but none of us had the gall to ask him.

About fifteen hands later there came another loud rip. This time Slim was raking in a pot, his A-K of hearts having combined with the three hearts that had flopped on the table. I glanced over and saw that another of Alexander's pockets hung from his shirt.

This time, the young man leaned over and said, "Don't let this bother you, Doyle. I'm just a mite superstitious. That's why I don't let nobody call me by my short name."

I said, "You mean, you think it's bad luck for anyone to call you—!"

"Don't say it!" he warned nervously.

"I wasn't going to," I lied.

70 Cardoza Publishing

I noticed that Slim was picking up on this conversation, trying to find some way to take advantage of this new information.

"Anyhow," Alexander continued, "my short name's always been bad luck for me. I called my papa in Toronto and told him how bad I was running. He said all I had to do is tear a pocket every time I saw a poker hand I liked. Then those hands will come back to me sooner or later."

He paused to rip another pocket because a full house had won a pot. "I'm not sure it'll work," he explained, "but it won't hurt to try. I had my girlfriend sew this shirt up special."

Now he asked to be dealt in. His luck was pitiful, but he kept tearing pockets. Some of us who'd been around poker a lot of years could sense this kid was getting really apprehensive. Obviously, the few thousand he had on the table represented the last of his bankroll.

Slim seized the opportunity to throw a bluff at him, knowing that a man is mighty reluctant to call a bet that will put him out of action. Alexander hesitated for a long time. As long as it looked like the kid was going to pass, Slim said nothing. But the second the kid looked at his small stack of chips, preparing to call, Slim said, "What do you do, Alex?"

Hearing the name Alex, the kid trembled and flung his cards away. "I quit! I told you never to call me that name!"

He stormed off to play blackjack. You've never seen a more ridiculous looking poker player. There he went, wearing a patched-together shirt with about thirty pockets and almost all of them torn off.

My advice to gamblers is to stick to percentages and steer clear of superstition. There may be such a thing as ESP, and when a decision is so close that I can't use scientific poker knowledge to resolve it, I generally go with my feelings.

But that isn't the same as superstition. I've always felt the most expensive thing a man can bring to the poker table is a rabbit's foot.

PART IV:
Advice at the Table

"Know how to win before you sit down. Experience may be the best teacher, but it's also the most expensive."

 **14** *Calling: The Right Motive*

You should only call a bet when you think the odds are big enough to earn you a profit. Maybe that sounds obvious, but you'd be surprised how often a man will call for the wrong reasons.

Here's something that happened a few years back. There are only two characters in this poker story. I'll call one Clarence, because I can't remember his real name. I only played with him one night at the Dunes, and he hasn't been around since.

The other I'll call Pete, which isn't even similar to his real name. Since he's a player with a very high reputation, it's better that he not be identified.

Now Clarence was one of those pretentious types who came long-striding into a poker room every now and then. He wore a cowboy hat, glossy boots and a belt with too big a buckle. There's not a soul in Texas who would take this guy seriously.

He slowed down his walk as he approached our table.

We were playing no-limit hold 'em, four-handed. Clarence said, "I'm from Florida, and I come to play poker." His voice was too dramatic, so I figured he'd practiced this line a hundred times in front of a mirror. He tipped his hat and stared ahead without smiling. His voice didn't sound real to me. Maybe he was forcing his tone deeper than felt comfortable to him.

"You came to the right place," said Pete, throwing his own

voice very low in sarcastic response. Everyone laughed and Clarence reddened slightly.

About twenty minutes later, it became clear to me that Clarence didn't know a lick about hold 'em. Erratic is the word that best describes his play. Sometimes he would throw away hands too cheaply and at other times he'd ride a hand clear to the end when he had no business playing in the first place.

All the while, he was spilling out these ridiculous lines about what his Pappy taught him. Lord, this guy was trying to be Maverick!

"Pappy said if a man can't look you in the eye, you should call his bluff," said Clarence, calling a very large bet by Pete.

Well, Pete just blustered around a bit about how, "It don't mean nothin' if I look you in the eye or not. Sometimes I got it and sometimes I don't. This time I don't, so you take the pot. But it don't mean nothin'.'"

Later, Pete's three kings were beaten when Clarence made a small flush on the last card.

"Pappy said poker is just two things: Gettin' good cards and playin' good cards," sighed Clarence as he raked in the chips.

Five minutes later he fired a $5,000 bluff into Pete. This time Pete had three aces. Without hesitation, he turned the two aces in his hand face up on the table and passed proudly. There were four diamonds on the board, and you had to figure Clarence for the nut flush.

That was bad figuring. Clarence gloated, "Pappy says if a man is courteous enough to show you his hand, you should show yours too." And with that he turned up his hand, a 10 of clubs and a 6 of hearts. Not even a pair!

Next, Clarence rattled on and on about that bluff and how he knew Pete was going to pass. "Pappy says you can always tell when it's the right time to bluff."

Over the next two hours, Clarence gradually got broke. He

left the game walking less proud than he'd come. He muttered something about getting more money and being right back, but he never returned.

Everyone had won a piece of Clarence's $50,000 disaster except Pete. To the best of my recollection, Clarence never bluffed except that one time when Pete had laid down the best hand.

The rest of us knew better than to call the "cowboy's" big bets. But Pete, well, he just kept right on calling . . . and losing.

I asked him about it later. Know what he said? "I'll be darned if I'll let that dude bluff me again and then spout off about how his Pappy told him to do it!"

So, you see, Pete was calling for the wrong reasons. Not calling because he wanted to make a profit, but calling because he didn't want to be embarrassed. Make sure you never make that mistake.

There's another bit of advice I want to add here: If ever a stranger makes a big issue of displaying a hand that he bluffed you with, it's pretty certain that he's not planning to bluff you again in the near future.

15 Don't Take a Bluff Personally

You might have heard the classic poker gag about the college kid who sends an urgent letter: "Dear Mom. Please send more money 'cause nobody's going to bluff *me!*"

Maybe that's worth a chuckle and maybe it isn't. There's a lot of sad truth in the joke. Treating a bluff emotionally is one of the most common and costly mistakes a poker player can make.

You'll see grown men get bent out of shape after being bluffed out of a pot. They start playing angry poker instead of rational poker. Often, the result is catastrophic.

Not only does the victim lose money in an ill-advised attempt to even the score, but also the bluffer often suffers because he's *expecting* revenge.

I use the following story frequently to illustrate this point. I call it "Winky and the Weasel" because those really were their nicknames. Winky was a mild-mannered older man—sort of an amateur psychologist who sat back quietly and studied his poker opponents. On this particular evening, there had been more than a few squabbles. One argument had nearly come to blows and several decks of cards had been torn up in anger.

One of the confrontations involved a jacks-or-better pot in which a young salesman, holding merely a pair of sevens, bet into the Weasel who laid down aces-up (or so he claimed). The young man showed his hand, probably thinking it was a good advertisement. The Weasel, a surly man in his fifties, promptly blew up, shouting, "Why don't you play like a man!"

Following that outburst, the Weasel's game quickly deteriorated. Half an hour later, already having blown back his profits, he tried to bluff the salesman out of a seven-stud pot. He got the salesman out of the pot okay, but Winky had made two pair on fourth street and just kept calling. The Weasel continued to bet right through the last card, whereupon Winky decided his two pair was too small to justify a call.

As soon as Winky folded, the Weasel showed a busted flush, paying tribute to his ego, which had earlier been damaged by the salesman's bluff.

Winky, realizing he was an innocent victim of someone else's ego war, leaned back calmly and looked the Weasel in the eyes. Then he quietly announced, "Gosh, I guess I'll have to get even with you before the night's over."

Those are the kind of words which, when uttered softly, can really unnerve another human being.

Well, the game just dragged on and on. The Weasel called almost every bet that Winky made, but every call was a loser.

After the game broke, I reminded Winky, "You said you were going to get even with the Weasel."

"I did get even—I never bluffed." I thought that over and it made a lot of sense.

In the world of poker, many a man takes bluffing too personally. The average guy will seek to avenge a bluff. More than that, after he himself has bluffed a pot he expects retaliation. Often he'll pay off every one of your bets just to ensure that you won't get even.

In that case, the cruelest poker weapon you can use is not bluffing.

16 Count 'Em While You Can

Half the poker players in America think you shouldn't count your chips while you're sitting at the table.

It's not just because Kenny Rogers made that line popular in his song, "The Gambler." That expression has been around for many, many years. While many occasional players feel that counting chips brings bad luck, every professional I know has a good idea how much money he has in front of him at all times.

There are some practical reasons for counting your chips at the table. Knowing how much you're winning or losing is like knowing the score of a football game. If you were a coach, you'd use the score as a tool to plan your strategy. This is somewhat true for poker, too, because your opponents often measure their moves by how you're doing. One example is that they may bluff more when you're losing. You certainly want to know what they know, and more accurately, if possible.

More importantly, you might want to count your chips to help evaluate your performance.

Perhaps you have a money goal in mind and intend to quit if you win it. Certainly you'd need to count your chips in that case.

Sometimes in big games, a player may sell pieces of his action. In that case, you'd want to know what your stack measures if someone phones in to see how his investment is doing.

Another reason for counting chips at the table applies mostly to no-limit. It's difficult to plan an offense if you don't know how much you can be raised or how much a reraise could cost you if you bet. For this reason, you always want to know how much money you have in front of you and how much your opponents have.

I remember playing hold 'em in Houston when a young man brought up the chip counting issue between hands. Kentucky John was auditing his stack when the kid said, "Don't do that! It will bring you misfortune."

At this point the kid was running very lucky and had turned a $100 buy-in into a disorganized mountain of chips that must have totaled $5,000. So John said, "Counting your chips is just part of the game, son."

"No it isn't. Not while you're sitting at the table. Every poker book in the world will tell you the same thing. If you don't believe me, ask anyone." He looked around the table for support, but the other players just grumbled noncommittally.

Well, things got real bad for the kid after that. First there was this hand where he started off with queens in the pocket, flopped a set and then promptly lost to a flush.

After a couple more bad bets, he placed a good luck penny on top of his stack, but that coin just followed his chips straight down to the cloth.

Pretty soon this previously good-natured lad was throwing cards and cussing at everyone. He didn't say anything more about counting chips because he was too busy whining about his misery. Finally the end came and he rose from the table sad and shaken.

You could see John debating with himself about whether to speak. Finally he couldn't resist. His eyes twinkled mischievously as he addressed the kid who was slinking out the door. "Now I see what you mean about not counting chips at the table. If you wait, they're a lot easier to count, aren't they?"

17 *Power Poker*

"You oughta read this book," Carl told me. "It's all about poker, and it shows you how to win big."

This was in my junior year at Hardin-Simmons University, and I hadn't yet mastered the art of winning consistently. So I took the book from Carl's hand, intending to give it a thorough reading.

Well, in those days I was taking basketball pretty seriously because several pro teams had shown an interest in me. Between studies and basketball practice, there wasn't much time to delve into a poker book.

In fact, by the time I got around to opening it, a fair amount of dust had gathered.

I can't remember the title exactly, something like *The Learning Experiences of a Poker Master*. It was a medium-thin volume.

The master kept emphasizing the same thing over and over: Play tight. He said that poker was like fishing: You wait and wait.

Even when you get the hand you're waiting for, you don't just barge into a pot, he explained. You sort of creep in cautiously. Maybe he thought this was the sort of practical, no-nonsense advice that would send his readers to the table crackling with electric excitement.

To me . . . well, I figured if I had to play that kind of

poker to win, I'd rather stay home and throw paper wads at my wastebasket.

Back then, all poker books preached that extreme patience was the ultimate poker weapon. Maybe that's worth a few chips in easy neighborhood games, but it won't win much money, and it won't earn anything at all against strong opponents.

Years later I considered sitting down and writing a book about the real secrets to winning: The kind of strategy that corrals all the chips on the table. After I won the world championship in 1976 at Binion's Horseshoe Club, a few people began to ask me to put a book together. I stalled. When I was fortunate enough to win again in 1977, I figured the time was right.

I chose five specialists to work with me, each the world's leading authority on one particular kind of poker. They were: Bobby Baldwin, "Crazy Mike" Caro, Chip Reese, David Sklansky and Joey Hawthorne. The first thing I did was to invite them one at a time to my home in Las Vegas where we taped everything they knew about poker.

If you think any one of them ever mentioned sitting and waiting as a key to successful poker, guess again. What was stressed over and over was dynamic, aggressive poker.

That's why, in promoting the book, I coined the term *Power Poker*. It means pressing your advantage. Chips go flying toward your opponent so fast that before long, unless he's a world-class player, he's totally bewildered and thoroughly beaten.

Of course, I don't advise you to give excessive action with inferior hands. But, whenever possible, you should seize the initiative. Make your opponent relate to you as the force to be reckoned with.

Warning: In order to use Power Poker, you must first have complete knowledge of the game you're playing. You've got to know the mathematics and the correct strategy.

When you apply Power Poker in this way, it takes about

twenty minutes to destroy an opponent. It's a three-step process:

1. Opponent becomes confused. "Why am I being raised so frequently?" he wonders. He tries to relate to the sudden bombardment and adjust his game, but there's no time to think.
2. Opponent is in shock. The bets and raises keep coming at him. From his point of view, it's cruel and relentless. You've tied psychological knots too complex for him to untangle. Now all his mental energy is directed toward you. What will you do next? He's scared. He can't make critical decisions about his own cards, because all his brainpower is used up worrying about what you're going to do!
3. Opponent stops raising. It's all over now. He looks, feels and acts beaten. He won't raise with anything less than a super hand because he's too afraid of your reraise. You will soon own all his chips. You have brought him to his knees.

Let me say once more that you must first understand the value of your hands so that when you push them to the limit, you're doing so with the odds in your favor.

As a matter of interest, I can think of an exception to the above.

During a World Series of Poker tournament, I was playing $600-limit heads-up hold 'em against a millionaire from Canada. We'd set up an unusual structure where there was only one blind, and it was the full $600. It quickly became apparent that this fellow wasn't going to call frequently enough to win no matter what.

I was winning about $25,000, but I had an appointment. Reluctantly, I was going to have to quit.

Along came "Crazy Mike" Caro.

"Play my chips for me. I've got to leave for about an hour."

In response, Mike leaned over and whispered, "I don't play hold 'em."

So I whispered back, "Just raise every chance you get."

He shrugged and took my chair. Well, telling "the Crazyman" to go ahead and raise every pot is like telling your kids to open their Christmas presents.

My Canadian opponent seemed relieved that he was going to play against someone else, but his comfort lasted only a few seconds. Mike immediately gave him a two-fisted overhand raise, cackling, "I make it more!" with his typical maniacal theatrics.

An hour later I returned to find him sitting alone at the table, mountains of chips stacked haphazardly in front of him.

"I assume you busted him," I smiled.

"Sure, Doyle. Hold 'em's easy."

If you're against weak players who are easily intimidated, and you can't decide whether to raise or merely call, just remember: when in doubt, raise.

18 Why Raise the Limits

No matter where you're playing poker, there's always someone who wants to raise the stakes. Is this good or bad? It depends.

One of poker's great facts of life is that limits seldom get bumped up more than double at a time. If you're playing nickel limit with a one-cent ante, the game will often get boosted to dime limit, but seldom more. A $5 limit game frequently goes to $10 limit. You might be playing $100 limit and the whole table will agree to play $150 limit or $200 limit. But there's only one time I've ever seen a whole table agree to jump from $100 limit clear up to $500 limit.

It happened in a strange way. The seven-stud game at this country club near Dallas began one morning at a semi-friendly $20 limit. Come about ten o'clock, Manny, five other big-limit players and myself showed up for golf. Poker usually came after dark. Suddenly there's this god-awful thunderstorm sweeping down from out of nowhere. Within two minutes the first fairway was a muddy swamp and electric golf carts were speeding toward the clubhouse.

So Manny asked, "Gin or poker?"

"Poker," is my vote, and all of the other regulars agreed.

Well, like I said, there was already a game in the card room, using up the only available poker table. Since the $20 limit was considerably below what most of us were used to, I didn't protest when the others took all four of the empty seats.

About a half-hour later, Manny got his seat, and there were only two of us still left out. As Manny left me sitting on the sidelines, he said, "Now there's five of us and three of them. Guess it's about time to up the limits."

"Just how far do you expect to up it?" I asked skeptically. After all, we were pretty much outsiders here. In fact, all of us were invited guests except Manny, who was a charter member.

"About 2,400 percent," was Manny's reply.

While I was doing the mental calculations that told me a 2,400 percent increase would make it a $500 limit game, Manny was beginning to lobby for higher stakes even before he played the first hand.

Nobody grumbled, so the game became $40 limit. There was one player in particular, Tom, who had been playing every pot. I don't mean almost every pot, either. What a rush this guy was having. I'll tell you, brother, I'd just seen him call the last two bets against three aces showing, catch two perfect straight-flush cards and knock off aces-full. Now that's what I call running good.

Pretty soon the stakes moved clear on up to $100 limit. Two of the original three players quickly got broke, leaving the seven of us up against the wild-eyed Tom, who was winning almost $10,000.

"Everyone ready for 500 limit?" Manny wanted to know.

Several of the boys just snickered, wondering how Tom would react to this. In the last three rounds, a total of twenty-four hands, he only missed playing twice.

Well, I expected to hear the words, "That's a little steep for me, boys," or "You fellas go ahead and play; I've gotta be gettin' on home." Instead, Tom said, "How much do we ante?"

Then came the great change. Tom was no longer playing almost every hand. He began choosing hands selectively and playing a style that was darn close to professional. By two in the afternoon when he quit, he was winning close to $80,000.

"Did you see how that guy tightened up?" Manny moaned after Tom left.

"He didn't just tighten up, brother," I argued. "He played mighty fine poker."

"You talking about Tom Arnold?" said a club member who had been an off-and-on spectator ever since we arrived. "Heck, he's the best local player around. Ain't played in a year or so, but I'm surprised you boys never heard of him. He always plays crazy for small stakes, 'cause he just don't have no patience for it. But you jack it up to $500 limit and you're in for some serious poker from Tom."

That's not atypical, either. I think most players handle themselves poorly when the stakes are less than what they want. But that isn't the only principle to keep in mind when you consider whether or not to raise the limits.

Here are some fairly absolute rules you should consider:

1. When an average player is in a limit higher than feels comfortable to him, he will usually play tighter than he should. This means, you'll make money by bluffing him.

2. When an average player is in a limit lower than he's accustomed to, he will usually play looser and far below his capabilities. This is why many superior players will lose consistently when killing time at lower limits.

3. When a very loose player is forced to play higher stakes than he feels comfortable playing, he often becomes a much better player. That's because, very often, he stops playing hopeless hands and ends up playing almost appropriately.

4. When a very tight player is forced to play higher stakes than he feels comfortable playing, he usually becomes even tighter. This is to your advantage, since you can usually run over too-tight players. By forcing them to play bigger, you're magnifying their faults.

5. If a game is very loose, it usually works against you to raise the limits. You should often keep the limits low and play conservatively.

6. If a game is very tight, it usually works in your favor to raise the limits and play aggressively.

Although I'm advising you to keep these things in mind, I confess to a tendency to raise the limits no matter what. Maybe this is because I'm basically a no-limit player, and often the more pressure you can put on an opponent, the easier it is to control him.

19 No Feel for No-Limit

"Texas! You'll never catch me south of Jersey again," swore the young man from New York. He began stuffing the pitiful remainder of his $10,000 bankroll into his pockets. It was less than $500.

Two days earlier he flew to Fort Worth. At two in the afternoon he came striding proudly into a semi-private poker room known informally as Pete's Parlor. It was named in honor of the owner of an adjoining restaurant through which anyone had to pass en route to the card tables.

Pete, of course, had a financial interest in the operation. His main function was to screen anyone entering the gambling arena. Most uninvited players were turned away at the door.

The New Yorker, though, talked himself inside. It happened to be on a day when some mighty powerful poker talent gathered. Amarillo Slim, Puggy Pearson, Johnny Moss, Sailor Roberts and myself were all present, having attended a party in Dallas the night before.

So, as I was saying, the guy entered the room taking big proud strides and flashing his wad of hundred-dollar bills in one hand. I guess he thought we'd never seen that kind of money before. Mainly we just yawned.

"I came to play."

"Sure, pull up a chair," Slim said. "It's no-limit hold 'em, the blind is . . ."

"What's the buy-in?" the young man interrupted.

Let me tell you, brother, this kid had picked an awful tough spot for himself. Besides the players I've already mentioned, the best in the world at that time, there were two local businessmen who weren't slouches, either.

"I'm Rick," said the newcomer, making a spectacle of shaking everyone's hand. "They call me Rochester Ricky. No hard feelings, win or lose?"

The tone of his question suggested that he couldn't fathom the possibility of a loss. We dealt him in.

Slim kept badgering him about what kinds of poker he was used to playing. Turned out to be a wide variety, including hold 'em. You got the impression that he pictured himself as the Rochester champion out to make good in the Texas big league.

Teasing him along, Slim dragged out all the information he could. Ricky talked and talked, seeming flattered by the questions, unaware that the more he spoke, the more we were able to gauge his game.

Pretty soon it occurred to me that he never mentioned no-limit. He kept using phrases like, "so I bet the twenty-dollar limit" and "the bet was fifty after the draw" and "after the flop you had to bet forty" and so on. That's when I knew this guy wasn't prepared for the high-pressure, psychological battle he had stumbled into.

If further evidence were needed, it came when he made a $400 losing call against Moss. He turned to me and said, "I didn't expect to win that one, but the pot was offering me two to one. It's worth a call in the long run, don't you think?"

That pretty well illustrates why limit poker players fare so dismally in no-limit situations. It's true that pot odds provide valid information about whether or not you should call a pot.

If there's $100 out there and it will cost you $20 to call, then you can lose five times for every time you win and still break even. That means your hand can be a 5 to 1 underdog and still be strong enough to justify a call. This happens again and again in limit games.

Where Rochester Ricky miscalculated was not in saying that he was getting 2 to 1 odds in calling Moss. He rightly reasoned that he needed to win only one out of three times in similar situations. What he didn't realize was that the hands which would have won one time out of three in limit games would not win nearly so often in no-limit.

You need stronger hands to call in no-limit, even if the pot odds are the same as they were in a limit game. Sound crazy?

Well, look at it this way: In limit poker, the bettor has the assurance that the worst that can happen is he'll get raised the same amount as he just bet. That's certainly no disaster.

What about no-limit? In the hand that Ricky had commented on, Moss had bet the size of the pot: $400. Johnny didn't have the luxury of knowing that the most he could get raised was $400. In no-limit games, you're faced with the ominous possibility that a man might move all-in at any time.

If your game is limit, and you want to try no-limit, keep these three things firmly in mind:

1. You need stronger hands to bet.
2. You need stronger hands to call or raise.
3. Bluffing is a much more powerful weapon.

The last point is very important. I've known limit players who won consistently but almost never bluffed. If you're going to have success at no-limit, you *must* know how to bluff. You've got to learn to intimidate your opponents in such a way that the mere threat of a bluff keeps them in line.

Even skillful no-limit players frequently make mistakes when they try to adjust to limit games. Most never make the transition because they're used to judging an opponent on the basis of, "Does he have me beat or doesn't he?"

Players get in this habit because no-limit bets tend to be large in relation to the size of the pot. A bet exactly the size of the pot is fairly standard.

When a man wagers an amount equal to the pot, he's risking the same money he hopes to win. For that reason, many no-limit players tend to call final bets about half the time.

Texans have gained a reputation as the best no-limit players. It's hard to quarrel with that when you consider how many world champions have sprouted from Texas soil. They'll tend to look you straight in the eyes, study you for a few seconds and call or pass on the basis of whether they think they're more likely to win or lose.

That's the problem. Put these same players in a limit game and they might continue to make their decisions in this manner. In limit, however, once you're committed to a hand you should call most of the time! The reason is this: The pot is usually proportionately large when weighed against the size of the bet.

In limit games, you must bet more often and call or raise more liberally. Keep in mind that bluffing will be a much weaker strategic tool. Most no-limit players bluff too often in limit games.

Basically, I like the drama of no-limit competition. Limit is more mechanical; it affords less chance for the superior player with "heart" to bury a weaker competitor.

Whichever game you're playing, remember the differences I've pointed out. Very few players can make the transition from one style to the other, but you'll be on the right track.

What about Rochester Ricky?

I'll always remember his parting words. "If you guys are ever in Rochester, don't bother to look me up. You won't see me playing hold 'em against Texans as long as I live."

We never saw him again. Too bad. The kid showed a lot of spirit. He might have made it.

20 *Weird Games, Real Money*

I've always had mixed emotions about wild-card games. It's just human nature, I guess, for a person to like to play games he's familiar with. No-limit hold 'em is my best game. Sometimes I wished that every time I got invited to a private game, the only thing they would deal was no-limit hold 'em.

Life isn't like that, and maybe it's a good thing. They tell me that, in the world of medicine, the day of the general practitioner is gone. This is the age of the specialist.

Well, in poker it's just the opposite. The day when a world-class player could name his own game is pretty much over. The true expert must be able to play a wide variety of poker games.

Remember, the greatest share of your poker knowledge is adaptable to all games. Learn to be versatile and you'll earn a lot more money.

* * *

During my college days in Texas, I used to play regularly with this kid nicknamed Professor Math. He managed to be obnoxious in a quiet sort of way, even though he wanted to be popular. You know the type—quick to comment at the table any time he saw a play that he judged to be mathematically incorrect. Helpful, really helpful!

There's probably nothing worse at a free-spirited, friendly home game than for some idiot to come along and ridicule his opponents for too liberal play. Professor Math had a habit of doing this all the time.

Tonight was a dealer's choice game. We'd been meeting regularly once a week, going into the second month. So far, the games chosen had been pretty conventional: hold 'em, jacks-or-better, seven-stud, five-stud and lowball draw.

Then this big burly lad named Scotty chose seven-stud with deuces wild. He began dealing. Now, let me explain that Scotty wasn't even a student. He was a custodian who fell into our group. Why or how he first got invited, I can't even remember. Anyway, he was known for short flashes of temper. Compared to the puny Professor Math, he was a giant. You get the picture?

All right. Just as P. M. was about to receive his first down card, he leaned back in his chair, folded his arms smugly and whined, "Deal me out."

"You quittin'?" Scotty wanted to know.

"No. Just relaxing. I don't play deuces wild."

The pot grew big. There was lots of laughter and lots of action. As is the case in so many home games, the mood had been set for more of the same. The next dealer declared, "Same game with deuces and fours wild." Defiantly, P. M. sat out this hand also. I still recall this pot. I won it with trip deuces and two fours, which normally would've been a full house. In this case it was five aces!

Like I said, I've got mixed emotions about wild-card games. In one sense, they tend to bring out the gamble in your opponents. They often create a carnival excitement in which players give away a lot of money painlessly. On the other hand, it's hard to calculate a correct strategy for a game that the dealer has just invented.

It was my deal now, and I decided to inject sanity into the game by selecting hold 'em.

"Deal me in," said Professor Math. This turned out to be a pot of medium size, which he won.

Now it was his deal. "Seven-stud," he decided. "Anything wild?" Scotty quizzed.

"No."

"Then deal me out."

Everyone laughed. Then, taking Scotty's cue, we all said, "Deal me out," in turn.

P. M. seemed stunned for a moment. After several seconds he took the deck and slammed it in front of the next dealer. "You deal," he sighed.

The point was made, and that could very well have been the end of it. But it wasn't.

Scotty rose to his feet looking meaner than ever. The rest of us were still laughing, but the big man showed no trace of a smile. "You can't pass the deal." he insisted. He handed the deck back to P. M.

So, solemnly, P. M. began to deal. He had very pale skin, and his face really showed the red of his embarrassment. Poker does not make good solitaire. He dealt himself his first card face down.

"You forgot to ante," Scotty snarled.

P. M. started to murmur something in protest, then glanced at Scotty, seeking some sign of good humor. Finding none, he anted. Then he dealt himself a second down card, then one up.

As he started to deal another card up, Scotty barked, "Wait! Don't deal yet; it's your bet. Let's see some action!"

Shrugging his shoulders, P. M. bet five dollars. When the farce finally ended, he raked in his own pot, worth over $100. He played a meek, losing brand of poker the rest of the night. There were a lot of wild-card games selected, and P. M. never asked to be dealt out.

There is lot of give and take in poker. Just to get a game in motion requires cooperation. Players who always want things their way find themselves unpopular in private games.

You have to remember that poker is often more than just a game of strategy and mathematics. It can be a game of public relations, too.

21 Bluffing: The Pride and the Panic

"You're losing your touch, Doyle." Kelly spat these words boastfully as he turned his hold 'em hole cards face up on the table. They were 9-8 off suit. Mine had been 6-4 suited, but I'd thrown them away when, before the flop, Kelly fired an unexpected $5,000 wager into a $330 pot.

Excitement rippled through the private card room in Corpus Christi. It was 1971, and I'd never experienced the huge galleries now associated with the World Series of Poker at Binion's Horseshoe Club in Las Vegas.

For some reason, there were about twenty onlookers gathered about the table. Almost all were relatives and friends of the players. In those days, spectators were almost unheard of. Usually the only ones were those who were waiting to join the game or those who had unfortunately got broke.

Kelly was a favorite of this crowd. His wife was there and so was another couple that I judged to be his friends. The three applauded when Kelly displayed his 9-8. I smiled as best I could. It just plain wouldn't have done any good to say, "That's the best hand." What difference did it make? Who cared? You win or lose depending on whether you cash out more chips than you started with. Whether you laid down the best hand or the worst hand doesn't matter, as long as you used good logic and good judgment.

Any man willing to fire $5,000 to win $330 can figure he's

going to win most of the time. What he's most worried about is getting his $5,000 raised and having to surrender all that money without even seeing the flop. That hadn't happened to Kelly yet, but the time would come.

A few hands later, Kelly scrutinized the fifth board card and then bet $3,000 into me and one other player. I could tell he was just crying for a call, so I folded two pair. The other man called and Kelly raked in a sizable pot on the strength of his three queens—two in the pocket, one on the board.

"You escaped that time, Doyle." Clearly I was his target tonight. I didn't know why then, and I never have figured it out. It's just one of the things you learn to live with in big-stakes poker. Some nights somebody will come gunning for you when you least expect it. There's really not much you can do except play your cards.

About an hour later, I bet $2,000 with A-K. Kelly called and all others folded. The flop came 4-K-A. I bet light, $800, feeling Kelly might just be tempted to raise in light of his early comments about me. Sure enough, he jammed the pot $12,000. I didn't figure him for much, so I raised my whole stack. I know it's an overused expression, but Kelly really turned white. Up until that time, I never realized what "turning white" really meant.

It was time for me to get my jibe in for the night. After all, I'd taken some ridicule from Kelly, so fair's fair. I said the most obvious thing I could think of, considering the circumstances. "Hey, Kelly, you turned white. I guess this means you're going to pass."

Sure enough, only Kelly didn't just pass. He stood up trembling and flung his hand into the discards. "I think I better take a walk," he grumbled. His three followers in the mini-gallery seemed stunned. I smiled.

Kelly had just demonstrated one of the worst reasons a man can bluff: pride. Never let your ego take control of your actions. Poker is a game involving a lot of luck, and the road to winning is long and unpaved. It's practically impossible to prove who's the best player in a matter of hours, so the top professionals never try. They just count their profits at the end of the year.

There's another terrible reason to bluff. And when Kelly came back fifteen minutes later, he showed an example of this one, too. By now, his previously healthy stack looked like someone had fired a Confederate cannon into it. Lordy, it was pitiful what remained of his chips. He found himself involved in a pot with two nines before the flop. That ate up half his bankroll. Now, with just $4,000 left in front of him, he watched the flop come A-Q-J—one of the worst things that could happen to him. You had to figure that flop was likely to help his opponent, because a man would have needed something to invest $4,000 to see the flop. A pair smaller than nines was unlikely, so you had to figure the opponent held high cards and had paired.

Again Kelly turned white. This time he instantly bet his remaining money on the pitiful hope that his opponent would pass. Kelly hadn't even given himself time to think. His bet was simple desperation. It's what I call a panic bluff and it costs gamblers a lot of money every year.

Kelly was called. He lost the pot to aces and jacks and walked away whimpering. His wife held his arm as he left, and his two friends followed at a good distance.

I call the most common reasons for bluffing the "Three Ps of Poker: Pride, Panic and Profit." Profit only sounds good to me.

22 Working Hard to Win a Call

They say a man who sits on the fence, unable to decide whether to call or pass, can often be prodded into calling. I reckon this is so, but sometimes you need to work extra hard for that call.

Once I was playing with someone named Runty, who was actually about five-feet-eleven, so you wondered how he got nicknamed. We were playing no-limit five-card draw. Runty, he was a real talker. Sometimes you figured there was a motive for what he was saying, such as an attempt to bolster a bluff or induce a bad call. But other times you knew he was just babbling because he didn't know how to stop.

I was about twenty-eight at the time, a good player but not nearly as card-wise as I would later become. Maybe I was immune to most of the tricks and tactics that players had up their sleeves, but I could still be steered in the right direction if it was done tactfully.

On this particular hand, I'd drawn to a pair of aces and caught a third ace. Runty, who was the opener, had drawn one. He checked, so I bet $200. Runty hesitated before slamming a $500 raise at me.

My first thought was, *why didn't I just plain check and make things simple.* After all, this was no-limit, and a general principle is: In no-limit you need a more secure hand to risk a bet. That's because a man might just jack you out of your seat with a raise any moment.

After about thirty seconds of studying Runty, I was pretty convinced I should pass. If ever a man looked like he was hungry for a call, it was Runty. But just as I prepared to fling my three aces into the discards, he started that crazy babbling.

"Ah, come on Doyle, show some courage. No man ever got nowhere without taking a chance."

Of course, this made me even more certain that my best move was to pass. I wasn't in the mood to be conned.

But Runty kept right on at it. "Tell you what, Doyle. I'll leave my whole raise in there, but I'll let you call it for two-fifty. That's a half-price bargain."

It seemed pretty obvious to everyone that no man would let you call for half-price on a bluff. But for some reason, I didn't throw in my cards right away. Instead, I listened to his prattle.

"I know what you got, Doyle. You got yourself three jacks or something. Well, all I got's the same two pair I went in with."

Of course, I didn't believe that. I felt almost certain Runty had a full house, but now I began to wonder. What if he really did feel I had three jacks? Now, suppose he had disguised his hand to begin with, drawing one to three of a kind. In order for him to want a call, he'd need to have a large set, say, kings or aces. Well, he couldn't have three aces, because those were mine.

So I thought, *if Runty had three kings, would he act the way he's acting now?* It seemed pretty reasonable that he would. But there were so many other likely hands he could be holding. It just wasn't worth the call.

Still, I wasn't ready to toss my hand in, so I offered, "Show me a card and maybe I'll call."

Quickly he flashed me the 6 of spades.

Even though I'd thrown away a 6, that didn't tell me enough so I grinned and said, "I need more information."

He cooperated by flashing an ace of diamonds.

Well, brother, in my whole life I don't believe I've pushed my stack into the pot any faster. He couldn't have four sixes, because I'd discarded a 6. He couldn't have sixes full because then he'd need a second ace. The very best hand he could have was three kings.

"What's wrong with you?" he shrieked. "How can you take all that time thinking about whether to call or not and then raise?"

For more than a minute, he kept staring at the pot. He was clearly undecided. He began to pass, but I said, "Runty, that pot seems mighty big to me." He hesitated. So I babbled on a bit until finally he shook his head sadly and called.

Sometimes a man needs a little prodding.

PART V:

Advice Away from the Table

"There's more to poker than playing cards"

23 Leave Your Personal Woes at Home

Nothing will bend a poker player out of shape as fast as a fight with his wife or girlfriend.

During my poker experiences, I've befriended a lot of up-and-coming players that looked like they were going to grab all the money in town, sweep it off the tables and rent a truck just to drive it home. Lots of times, I've taken a piece of some player I had a lot of respect for. Maybe it was only 10 percent, but sometimes I'd have more than half of a player I really respected who needed backing.

The one thing I just never did was take a percentage of a man who seemed emotionally upset. Lordy, I've seen guys slave for years, using the best discipline they could just to gather together an adequate bankroll.

Then something happens. I don't know what the causes are and I don't ask. The only thing that's for sure is: When a man's got something heavy on his mind besides poker, he's got no business playing.

You just can't make critical decisions when you're going through personal agony. My advice is to stay away from poker. And if you're going to take a piece of someone, make sure it's a player who doesn't have bad problems of his own.

The worst case of self-destruction I've ever seen happened six years ago to a kid named Craig. We used to call him "Super

Rock" because he just never got out of line in a poker game. Not only that, he'd select his games really carefully. Sometimes he just sat around the card room for days waiting for the right game. Waiting and waiting. The kid had incredible patience.

But he was also a ladies' man, and one day while he was sitting in a $100/$200 limit seven-stud game, in came this young lady all flustered and ruffled. She marched right up to Craig while he was in the middle of a hand and she threw some house keys into his pile of chips.

"Here!" she screamed. "Take these! Keep these, you miserable rat! I don't want them any more!" Then she stormed out.

Well, Craig just sort of shrugged it off like the young lady didn't mean a thing to him. Of course, that wasn't the case. You could see that he had inner turmoil that didn't match his cool exterior. He started to play really bad. Pretty soon he was throwing cards and cursing, things he'd never done before.

I sat in the game, got lucky right away and snatched a few pots from him. He was fuming. "Stupid broad!" And every time he lost a pot it was "stupid broad" this, and "stupid broad" that.

After a while he was peeling more bills from his money clip. Super Rock had become a "live one" and the limits kept getting raised and he kept losing. It took him five hours to unload the bankroll he'd taken over a year to accumulate.

Just about the time he got broke, his girl waltzed back into the poker room all smiles. She hugged him from behind and murmured, "I'm sorry. This whole thing's so silly."

And then Craig got up, broke and shaking, and his girlfriend asked him how he'd done.

All he could manage was, "Lost a little."

She said, "Well, honey, you know you shouldn't play when you're upset." Then they left together, and I haven't seen them since.

24 *Road Games*

Brother, it's hard enough to *play* poker in Las Vegas; I sure wouldn't want to *learn* poker in that town. By the time a pro feels comfortable enough to settle himself in Vegas, he should have already learned the ropes elsewhere.

Way back in the late sixties, I met up with a man named Carl. He was maybe seventy-five, but he still had his wits about him. Not a bad player, either. We were sitting at a sleepy cafe drinking coffee and trying to keep awake after an all-night session in El Paso. The talk was mostly about how hard the traveling was between poker games, although Carl rarely did the driving himself anymore. In fact, he'd got to winning so regular lately that he'd hired himself a full-time chauffeur.

Suddenly Carl changed the subject. "Doyle, ya been up to Vegas lately?"

Well, up until then I just never figured Las Vegas was a good idea. Those games around the Panhandle and down deeper into Texas were mighty sweet.

"What's in Vegas?" I wanted to know. Sure, I'd heard about the poker games in Nevada, but there weren't too many there at the time. Besides, I never heard of anyone getting rich off those games in the sixties.

"There are some fair games. Pretty tough, but big enough to be worth your while if ya can hold a few hands. I'd never of recommended Vegas to you a year ago, but you're just now reachin' a level where you might up and take them for a bundle of cash. What I'm saying is you gotta pay your dues on the road, and, Doyle, I think you've paid yours. Next time you feel the urge, take a trip that way and see what happens."

Well, I kept Carl's advice in mind, but I didn't try Vegas out for some time. When I did, Carl's words turned out to be true. The competition was mighty tough up there. In fact, they got me broke a couple times. It took me a while to work it through my head that these guys were playing more serious than some of the boys down in Texas.

Sure, we had tough competition down South. In fact, the greatest no-limit players in the whole world sprouted there. But mixed in with the pros was plenty of easy money. Those soft spots were sadly missing from the Vegas tables. Maybe there were some players giving it away, but I sure didn't find them. Trouble was, years ago, there just wasn't very much poker in Las Vegas. It hadn't caught on. At the top limits, there was mostly a bunch of hard rocks battling each other for the occasional weak player's bankroll.

A man could just about forget the smaller games. The rake was too high.

Today things have changed, but I still figure Carl was right. You need to get that experience under your belt before tackling Vegas. They're still plenty strong, even though you'll find some easy pickings, too. If you want to make a living, day in and day out, Vegas can be a land of poker promises. But I think a man should earn his way to Vegas, and those hot hold 'em games in Texas are still the best training ground I know about.

In Carl's words, "You gotta pay your dues on the road."

25 Being Too Proud of Your Bankroll

If you've ever driven across the middle of Texas, you know there can be long stretches between towns. Sooner or later some town will shoot up in your path. There's usually a gas station, some buildings, and a cafe.

You always enter the cafe because the long drive has made you feel tired and isolated.

It was in a cafe such as this where Red and I stopped. We were both in our mid-twenties, and this was the first time I'd ever traveled the poker circuit with him. Although we'd only toured together for six days so far, I could tell this would be our last week. Red was just a little too flamboyant for my tastes. And when you're on the road, you've got to get along perfectly with your traveling partner.

Our bill for lunch was $3.40 and it was Red's turn to pay. The cashier was a dreary looking woman of fifty. Red liked to keep his small bills tucked inside his wad of hundreds. Now he fanned through about $5,000 worth of big bills before locating the spending money.

The woman gaped. "You boys must be from Amarillo," she blustered. "They tell me there's a lot of money in Amarillo." I noticed that the woman wasn't the only one admiring Red's bankroll. Two husky, mean-looking kids, a few years younger than we were, stood several feet away and pretended not to be interested.

As soon as we got in my car, I chastised Red for flashing the money. "You're just asking to get hijacked!"

Hijacked is the word southern poker pros use for getting robbed. This was back in the sixties and big-league poker had its drawbacks in Texas. High-stakes games were often held up. You even heard rumors about players being assaulted with machine guns!

"Nobody's got the nerve to try anything around here," he projected. "This here's your typical friendly town."

As I drove beyond the city limits, it started to rain. Then it was pouring something fierce. My windshield wipers weren't very good and I couldn't safely travel more than twenty-five miles an hour. Through the intense throbbing sound of the storm, I could hear the pale honking of a car far behind us on the highway. The sound grew closer. Finally I saw another car behind me. Drifting toward the road shoulder, I slowed to twenty to let it pass.

"What do they want?" Red wondered.

"They just want to get by," I speculated hopefully.

No such luck. The other car came alongside ours and stayed there for several seconds. I recognized the man in the passenger seat as one of the two who'd been ogling Red's bankroll back in the cafe. Suddenly, he rolled his window down and pointed a large gun at my head. Trying to outrun their later-model car seemed imprudent. I pulled over.

It was a fast hijacking. No one got hurt. Red and I were tied up and left to grovel in the mud of a nearby field. I watched the other car pull away. It had Alabama plates, so those boys weren't citizens of the town we'd seen them in either.

Finally, I worked my ropes loose and untied Red. They'd got all our money except $550, which was kept in the glove compartment for emergencies.

Now $500 was just enough for one of us to buy into tonight's game. We did the only civilized thing that seemed sensible.

"Deal," Red barked. We'd already agreed that our partnership must be dissolved. The plan was to play one hand of showdown poker, the winner claiming the $500, the loser taking the remaining $50 to the nearest bus depot and purchasing a ticket home.

I'll always remember the hand, which was dealt between us on the front seat of the car. He looked mighty sad when I dropped him off at the next town, but I wasn't feeling sympathetic. I figured it was his fault we were in this predicament.

I tried to imagine Red at the bus depot, counting out the right amount for his ticket. Compared to paging through $5,000 earlier in the day, this must have been a humbling experience. I ended up winning more than $10,000 during the next week, so maybe the hijacking worked out for the best.

Gamblers sometimes need to carry a lot of cash, but I always thought that exposing money in a public place is pretty stupid. One thing's for sure: You can't flash a bankroll you don't have.

26 When Speculation Makes Sense

To a gambler, a lost opportunity is usually more expensive than a lost wager.

It's pretty hard to prove this, because when a man loses a $1,000 bet, he needs only to yank out his money clip, grumble a little and peel off ten $100 bills.

The debt is then paid, the agony short-lived and the amount of the setback is precisely engraved in memory. This kind of loss is measured by the bulge of your bankroll as you stuff it back into your pocket, weighed against how it used to feel.

But even the best gamblers suffer devastating losses from time to time without feeling the smallest bit of pain. How can that be? Let me share a poker experience of mine from many years ago so you'll be able to understand what I'm talking about. This happened in Abilene, but I could have selected any similar incident from among dozens that come to mind.

Toby was one of those companions that appears in a man's life and, for a period of months or even years, serves as an almost inseparable friend. Then you each drift down other roads and, one day, you awake and realize the relationship is gone. I haven't received even a letter from Toby in many years. Still, the friendship survives in my memory.

We were both struggling young gamblers at the time. I suppose our skills were nearly equal, although Toby had a tendency to be more adventurous. He'd gamble fairly big on horses, football, and even auto races. While my reputation certainly wasn't one of conservatism, he made me look staid and steady by comparison.

My friendship with Toby had blossomed into a full-fledged partnership in which we shared financially all our gambling results, the good and the bad.

Of late, Toby had almost forsaken poker for horseraces (betting through bookies because there were no tracks operating in the region) and a little gin rummy. His luck was so bad that, for the past two months, I'd virtually supported the two of us. My poker streak was something like twenty-five wins in the last twenty-seven plays.

This was one of those days where there wasn't a poker game to be found anywhere that I knew about, except the one that ran all the time at a ranch house north of town. It was a game for high rollers and I had neither the bankroll nor the prestige to be invited.

So Toby and I sat in an Abilene coffee shop, talking a lot about poker and a little about how he figured a man could beat the track simply by betting the favorite horses in the last two races each day. He reasoned that a lot of folks were good and stuck by the eighth race and were betting long shots in a desperate attempt to get even.

"Whatcha say Doyle? Toby?" The voice came from behind us, and we both turned to see Colonel Ed.

He was a local gambling maniac who owned half a dozen small businesses, but lost a good share of the profits at the poker tables. "Got a proposition for you boys," the fifty-ish man offered, flashing his crooked teeth and politely tipping his well-worn cowboy hat.

Toby gave me a conspiratorial nudge in the ribs beneath the padded divider that separated our booth from the Colonel's. The man was noted for his proposition bets and, while as a rule you shouldn't accept another man's hustles, many a

Texas gambler had padded his wallet accepting Colonel Ed's proposals.

The elbow in my ribs had been none too gentle, but I could understand Toby's excitement, so I forgave him.

"What do you have in mind, Colonel?" I inquired.

He brought his coffee with him and joined us in our booth. It took him only a minute to spell it out. It was this: He would play heads-up five-card draw poker against either one of us, a series of $1,000 freeze-outs at straight $50 limit. If he lost, he would pay the entire $1,000, but if we lost we had to pay only half—$500.

He concluded, "Here's the catch, gents. I get to look at five cards and if I don't like 'em, I get another complete five-card hand off the top of the deck. Then we draw."

I tried to analyze this proposal quickly, but there were several factors to consider. Would the Colonel play his usual weak game? How much of an advantage was it for him to be able to reject a hand before the draw and get a fresh five cards to start with? He was offering us 2-1 on our money. Was it worth it at that price?

"I'll leave you boys alone to talk it over. If you want to try it out at half the stakes and see how it goes, that's okay by me." He went outside for some fresh air.

The ensuing discussion between Toby and me went like this:

"I'm willing to give it a shot. What do you think, Doyle?"

"I can't figure my way through it without more time. Neither can you," I chided. "You're always ready to jump in head first without even checking whether the water's heated."

"Well, I'm for taking a chance."

"You're always for taking a chance, Toby. But I figure ol' Colonel Ed's probably got the best of this one."

"Let's find out."

"What do you mean, 'Let's find out?'" I wanted to know.

My thinking was that, for a gambler, finding out could be an expensive concept. Toby said, "We'll go along with it for $1,000 and, if we lose, we quit. I'll bet the Colonel's lost a hundred grand this year on his crazy propositions."

I thought for a while. Mostly I kept reminding myself that my share of our bankroll was only $3,000, and even a $500 setback would hurt. Colonel Ed, well, he could up and lose $50,000 and it wouldn't really damage his bank account.

Finally I made my decision. "I'm going to pass on this one."

"Well, I want to give it a try."

"All right, then go ahead, Toby. But you're on your own."

He seemed surprised. My image, even back then, was of a gambler who liked to investigate new frontiers. But that year had been particularly hard; a lot of ups and downs and times when I'd barely escaped getting broke. I felt good because, for once I'd made a sensible and conservative decision.

"I guess we aren't partners anymore," Toby shrugged, trying to seem matter-of-fact, even though it was painful for both of us.

"Guess not," I said.

So then it was up to Toby to go down to the back room of the pool hall with the Colonel to play poker. I tagged along as a witness.

Well, it didn't take long to see what was going to happen. Toby won the first freeze-out for $500. It would have cost him only $250 to lose, since the agreement was that he would get half his buy-in back.

While they were re-dividing the chips for the second $500 contest, I went into the poolroom to get some cokes from the counter. It took me maybe three minutes to order and pay for the drinks. When I returned, they were still dividing their chips.

Not exactly "still dividing," as I quickly learned. Toby had won another freeze-out in my absence. So now they began playing $1,000 tap-outs. I watched how the Colonel played a few hands. He should have had a great advantage because of the stipulation that he could exchange his first five cards for a new hand if he wasn't satisfied.

However, he was surrendering much of that edge by using poor strategy. Once, in fact, I saw him throw away a pair of jacks and try for a new hand. On the second deal he was forced to play a pair of fours and lost to two tens!

Oh, how I wished I had a part of Toby's action! But the partnership was dead, murdered by my own words and there was no use whimpering about it now.

The match went on all afternoon. Finally the Colonel said, opening his checkbook to write the last installment of what had proved to be a $35,000 loss, "That's enough for me."

He had surrendered to Toby the last of the $100 bills he'd brought with him. Now, with Toby walking out the door, he turned to me and withdrew three crumpled twenties from his wallet. "You might as well have these, Doyle," he mumbled, his spirit gone. "How about a little seven-stud?"

And that's how I ended up winning $60.

It was a sad lesson to learn, but it's something that's stayed with me through the years. I'm sure that, in the long run, the knowledge I gained that day was worth the $17,500 that would've been my share of Toby's win.

What I learned was: When you find yourself in a situation where you don't know if you have the best of it, it's often worth risking a small sum of money to investigate—particularly if the rewards are many times the amount you're planning to invest.

Sometimes I select a game where the competition looks terribly weak, but there's a small chance there might be cheating. Usually I'll just sit down with the minimum buy-in and see what develops. If the game is on the square, I'm figuring on a $20,000 profit. If not, well, I've wasted only $1,000. Those are pretty good odds.

Like Toby said that day in Abilene, "Let's find out." I can't remember anyone's words ever sounding so reckless and being so right.

27 The Library Robbery

When you travel from game to game down south, you have to safeguard yourself against hijackers. Now, the word hijacker might not mean the same thing to you that it means to a professional poker player. To the pros, a hijacking is an armed robbery. For a while, during the late sixties and into the seventies, it was kind of a jungle in Texas. Big-limit poker games had two problems: In some localities, the police were dead set against poker; and hijackers were apt to break the door down at any moment.

Being hijacked is no fun at all. You usually end up face down on the floor with some big old pistol rammed against your skull and some half-sane goon pillaging your pockets.

It got to be really bad. There were hijackings reported two and three times a month. We were all mighty fed up with it, but I wasn't prepared for the invitation I got to old man Don's game.

When I phoned him to see if he had a full table on the following Saturday, he said, "Naw, we got two seats left."

"Well, save one for me," I said. "I'm planning to be in your territory."

"Sure, Doyle. Just one thing—it's $20 limit."

That stunned me. Don had typically hosted one of the largest, meanest games in Texas.

"Well, I thought the game was no-limit, Don. Are the same people going to be there or what?"

"Yep. It's all the regular boys. And it is no-limit. What I mean by twenty dollars is that's all you can have in your pocket. Any man who comes with more than twenty bucks gets permanently barred from the game. I want the word passed around that Don's game ain't worth hijacking!"

Well, naturally I had my reservations. Playing on credit sometimes works and sometimes doesn't. But Don assured me that everyone could be trusted. The plan was to settle up the next day at the public library.

It all sounded pretty crazy to me. For one thing, you couldn't figure that a library was a heck of a lot safer than Don's house. Besides, what if the losers decided to oversleep or something? Wasn't this stretching honor a bit far?

Don said, "Don't worry. If anyone don't pay, I'll stand good for it." It was hard to argue, since the old man was both honorable and rich. The game on Saturday went about like I expected. Don carefully kept track of who had bought chips and how many. Players tended to gamble more heavily than usual, and whenever they got broke they just ordered up a new stack without hesitation.

When the game ended, I was winning a few thousand. Don was the big winner—almost $20,000—and there was only one loser, Phil, who owed $28,000.

The next day all but one of us promptly met at the library at 10 a.m. We had to be careful not to cause a commotion, because the librarian seemed suspicious. Some loitered about, flipping through books until it became pretty clear that Phil wasn't going to show. Maybe he got hijacked on the way to the library.

Don? Well, he just calmly checked out a book on checkers and had us follow him to the bank. He was out $8,000 plus the $20,000 he was owed. Next week the game was strictly cash again.

I always figured there were five great fears a gambler has to live with: getting broke, getting robbed, getting arrested, getting cheated and not getting paid.

28 Winning: It's a State of Mind

"I can't play until I prepare." Keith told me.

"Prepare how?" This tall young fellow from Reno had come down to Vegas about two weeks ago. Every day so far, he'd almost destroyed the seven-stud game at the Dunes.

He played pretty mean poker: solid yet aggressive. It was the kind of poker that could make you dizzy just watching it. One thing about his manner stood out in my mind: The kid had almost total confidence—like he knew he was going to win even before the first card was turned, even before the deck was shuffled.

Now, I'm not saying that you can win at poker just by *acting* confident. You've got to really *be* confident. You've got to feel it in your head and let it touch your soul.

When you feel that supreme ray of confidence radiate from within you, things will happen at poker tables that are almost magic. You'll reach way back in your mind and make terrific calls and great lay-downs. Everything will seem to fall together; everything will work in harmony. And you'll win like magic.

We've all seen it. Whenever a man sits down at a table, bound and determined to win and really believes he will win, his chances of success are greatly enhanced. He plays better, and because he does, he seems to bring himself good fortune.

That's why when a man who's capable of playing great cards gets on a winning streak, there's just no stopping him.

Keith was on a winning streak. I was just as determined to put an end to it as he was to have it continue. We'd agreed to start a four-handed game and, just as we were ready to deal, he'd told me he had to prepare.

He slipped down the aisle, past a crowded craps table and found the men's room. After a minute or so, I followed out of curiosity. There he was in front of a mirror, more intensity written across his face than you could imagine. He stared at himself for a very long moment, then a grimace crossed his lips and he said, "I will win!"

Then again, "I will win." And again and again, and each time his voice became smoother. Finally, in a totally controlled tone, he said, "Keith, you cannot lose!"

By now his posture had even become prouder and more erect. I left the men's room without being noticed. He came to the card room minutes later and, as usual, racked up the game.

Luckily, I managed to escape that night with a small win of my own. Well, we got to be friendly over the next week. He described the psychological maneuvers he used to psych himself up. They were fairly elaborate. But he kept experimenting, trying to find the perfect recipe. He said he was even "talking confidence" to himself before he went to bed at night.

I liked his attitude, and I confess I even tried some mental conditioning of my own; it seemed to work. Once he phoned and woke me up to see if I wanted a piece of his action. I sleepily agreed to take a third and by the time I woke up, he had scored $30,000. So that was an easy $10,000 for me.

But then his experiments got really bizarre. He'd stand up in the middle of meals at restaurants and spout, "Win! Win! Win!" until his voice was almost hysterical.

Well, needless to say, I didn't care to keep his company after that. Even though he was still on his winning streak, his mind was going fast. He told me how he'd discovered that "Everyone plays better when they're losing a little. Before I play, I've been pretending I'm down a few thousand. That way I play real tough poker trying to get even." That strategy seemed to work for him. Then one night he decided to pretend he was losing $100,000 from the start. He told me it was going to take some special mental effort to make himself believe it. He disappeared into the men's room for half an hour. When he returned, he looked like a wild man: Eyes glazed; totally disoriented.

"Deal me in! Deal me in! Deal me in!" he shrieked as he sat down at the table. The game was seven-stud, $300 limit, and a $100,000 comeback is a nearly impossible task. So there he was in a game where, according to his muddled mind, he had no chance of getting even.

He won the first pot, but instead of feeling victorious, he didn't seem to care. In his head he was still losing $98,000. His posture was slumped.

Well, he just went crazy, barging into pot after pot, breaking cards and cussing. His play became desperate and erratic, even when, at first, he was winning $12,000. It took him a day and a half of continuous play to unload his bankroll. But he managed to do it.

I'm a believer in using personal psychology to build your own confidence. The proper mental exercises can be great for your bankroll. Just be sure you're lifting your spirits and not playing tricks on your mind.

Cardoza Publishing 129

PART VI:
Strategy and Tactics

"A man with no money is no match against a man on a mission."

29 *Shifting Gears*

"You're in third gear, Doyle! Try using first."

This was my first driving lesson. The old Ford belonged to my teenage buddy who sat nervously beside me grumbling, "The clutch, Doyle, don't forget the clutch."

We were at a stop sign near the bottom of a hill. A horn blared behind me and I hurriedly struggled to obey my friend's instructions. Finally, I worked the stick into low gear, letting the clutch out unevenly as the car lurched forward and began to climb the hill. About half way up, I tried shifting to second gear, but the transmission groaned in protest.

My friend said, "Don't worry about second, Doyle. Sometimes it don't go in too easy. First and third is all you need anyway. First and third."

It's an incident that vividly survives in my memory. That's probably because it perfectly illustrates the one thing that separates an average professional poker player from a superstar: Superstars shift gears. More than that, they shift suddenly from first to third and back again, seldom using anything in between.

Shifting gears means playing super-aggressively, then changing to a slower, more selective game while your opponents continue to play according to the pace you've set. They're not aware that you've shifted—only you know for sure.

Well, I just can't emphasize how important this concept

is. Many skilled players realize the psychological advantage of varying the speed of their game, but they tend to play in long, fluid waves. They get slightly more aggressive hand by hand until, eventually, they reach a peak. Then they gradually ease up and play more conservatively until they reach a valley and slowly begin to open up again.

This isn't the right way to change speeds.

If this is how you've been playing poker, my advice is: Next time, shift suddenly. You'll instantly sense a new and dramatic power over the other players and your profit will be commensurate with their confusion.

A few years ago, I became pretty friendly with a lawyer named Bill. He was not a bad player, but he was too conservative: he never varied his game. You know the type: intelligent, but not much imagination when it came to poker.

We started a six-handed no-limit hold 'em game at the Dunes. Bill remained about even for the first hour, playing a solid but very predictable game. The rest of us sort of played around him. For the most part, we avoided confrontations when he held a strong hand.

Then, suddenly and unexpectedly, he bet $8,000 with a pair of tens, bluffing out an opponent who had at least aces. He even won a small side pot from an all-in player holding two eights.

A few hands later, he brought it in for $500, I made it $600, and he jumped all over this with a $7,000 raise. To this day, I still wonder if he was bluffing. I sat out the next hand and watched Bill begin with A-K in the pocket, flop a pair of kings and push the hand very aggressively, netting $8,000. There was nothing wrong with his play, mind you, but none of us expected this from him.

Certainly we didn't expect what happened within the next fifteen minutes. He was in almost every hand, firing his chips at us with a vengeance. Raise, reraise, jack it up, there just wasn't any end to it. He won a few, lost a few and was still roughly even. Suddenly, he became a poker tyrant with a world-class flair.

"Take it easy, Bill," I joked. "Give us a chance to breathe." I was just teasing, but maybe he took me seriously. For the next four hours, it was back to poker as usual. Whenever he got himself mixed up in a pot, he had a big edge. Since it took us a while to realize that he'd slammed on the brakes, we naturally gave him more action than he was entitled to.

By now he was racking up the game. It was due to a good run of cards and partly due to his new mastery of shifting gears.

Sure enough, he began to push his hands with a reckless regard for possibility, just when we'd figured he was back to his old solid self again. Soon afterward, he lapsed into a conservative waiting game. Then another blitz, followed by an hour of tight play. I just couldn't believe he was capable of playing so well. Never in all my years of poker had I seen anyone improve so much from one session to the next. He was against some of the toughest no-limit players in the world, and *winning!*

Because of his brief flurries of excessively liberal play, he was earning far more on his good hands than he would have normally. I was surprised to see him quit the game, seeming distraught. After all, he was a big winner. I didn't see him for a month after that.

"I'm starting to take poker more seriously," he told me upon his return to the Dunes. "Maybe you could give me a few tips that would improve my game."

"Bill, it seems that you don't need too many tips. Last time I played with you . . ."

He interrupted before I could complete the compliment. "Oh, that. Well, I wasn't myself that night. You know me; I've always had pretty good control. You never see me out of line, do you Doyle? I play a pretty steady game, don't you agree?"

"Well, yes. But that night you played especially . . ."

"I know. I know, I wasn't myself that night, and I'm sort of . . . well . . . ashamed of it. Had a bad fight with my wife, Daisy, and I learned my boy's flunking out of college. It just got to me, that's all. I was playing my normal game and, before I even knew what was happening, I was barging head first into every pot like a maniac."

"One good thing you did was . . ."

"Then I'd catch myself, scold myself mentally and play good cards again. But my mind would start wandering again and I'd find myself playing crazy. The last time I felt myself losing control, I decided to quit. I really got lucky that night. Things are all right at home now. Kid didn't flunk out after all. I'm back to playing my regular game."

Sure enough, Bill was back to his normal strategy. In fact, I never saw him play top-flight poker again.

When you shift gears effectively, it's a little like a man struggling for control. Except in Bill's case, it was a fortunate coincidence, and he wasn't aware of it. Done right, you know precisely *when* to shift and you hold complete control over your opponents.

Shifting gears is possibly the single biggest secret you should master if you want to play poker at the highest levels.

Sometimes when I play about as forcefully as any rational human being can, I hear a voice in my head. It echoes from out of my youth, saying, "You're in third gear, Doyle! Try using first."

When I change gears, I do so suddenly because the voice reminds me, "Don't worry about second, Doyle. First and third are all you need."

30 Adapting to the Situation

Flexibility is an important poker talent. Some people just don't have it, and that can be mighty expensive.

Believe me, knowing how to play your cards is a big subject. It's not just what makes a good hand; it's what makes a good hand *at the* time. I'll bet you've heard players say, "I knew he had me beat, but I *had* to call with three aces." Maybe not those exact words. But at some point or another, every experienced player will hear the song of similar words chiming in his ear.

Let me explain one concept that comes slowly and with great difficulty to some players. It is not what cards you have that matters, it's how your cards stack up against the cards your opponents are likely to be holding. If you start off a hold 'em hand with a pair of red eights in the pocket, you know you have a speculative hand. Chances are you're going to need some good fortune to rake in the money.

Well, suppose the flop comes 8-9-10 of clubs. At first you're going to like this flop, but the more you consider it, the more you realize that there's a hailstorm full of trouble here. If someone's holding J-Q, you need to make a full house or four of a kind to win. The same is true if someone has two clubs. Also, you'd better worry about just one other club falling on fifth or sixth street and about someone having three nines, or three tens. All this spells caution. If you're playing no-limit and you push in a big bet here, remember you'd sooner *not* be called. That's because any call is apt to beat you.

Now suppose, using the same example, that you make a medium bet and get a reluctant call. I'm pretty sure that your three eights is the best hand at this point, so when the fourth card is the ace of hearts, you still feel confident about your hand. That might be a good time to make a sizable bet.

But suppose you made that medium bet after the flop, trying to feel out your opponents and see where your three eights placed you. Now old Johnny Moss just up and charges right back at you with a bet four times the size of the pot!

Inexperienced players might just sigh dismally and start pushing their chips in automatically. In their minds they're replaying those same tired words, "I don't like it, but I've got to call with three eights."

Here's a little advice: You don't have to call. If I were to define the main difference between good players and poor players, it's that good players play their cards and poor players let their cards play them.

It's too bad. I've seen many smart players put themselves at the mercy of the cards. Poker is a game where you have control over your action. You never have to call; you never have to bet; you never have to raise. You *choose* to call; you *choose* to bet; you *choose* to raise. You are the master.

It isn't just that many folks fail to throw away losing hands; they also fail to call with winners. Maybe you've heard a draw poker player say, "I think you missed your hand. If I had more than a pair of jacks, I'd call you." Well, brother, if you figure a pair of jacks is the best hand, then just go right ahead and call.

If you do, you're likely to hear, "How could you call with just one pair?" That's a typical statement uttered by astonished players who feel you should play your cards instead of your situations. Poker is not a game where the value of a hand is determined by how high it is. Sometimes weak hands win and sometimes strong hands lose. Take a philosophical approach and try to decide how good your hand is at one given moment. Nothing else matters. Nothing.

So don't say: "I know I'm beat, but I've got to call with three aces." Say: "Since I know I'm beat, I'll throw these three aces away." You'll feel good about it in the morning.

 **31** *First Grade Hold 'Em*

Hold 'em is my kind of game. A lot of folks get really worked up about seven-card and lowball. While I always found those games interesting, hold 'em just grabbed me tight one day and it never has let me go. I think if someone invented perfect poker, a game jam-packed with suspense and excitement, I'd still prefer hold 'em. I grew up on it. There's something about the mystery of the flop that always intrigues me.

Just about the only game played regularly in Texas used to be hold 'em. Some people believe it shouldn't be the game used to decide the world championship because people in the North and East hardly ever play it. Maybe there was a time when that held true, but these days most regular players know about hold 'em. They play it in Kansas and Wisconsin, and I hear it's really big in New York now.

There are a few observations I think will help beginning players to survive their first battles, even against those legendary Texas masters. Most advice, including my own, tends to be much too technical for beginners.

In limit hold 'em, you should not fall in love with small pairs. The great illusion of hold 'em is that starting with a pair of sevens might be just as good as starting with A-K. After you've played a few weeks and burned up a few bankrolls, you'll quickly decide that small pairs are a lot like rattlesnakes in the prairie. You're apt to be bit really bad when you least expect it.

Another thing I always advise friends when they first play hold 'em is that a pair of jacks is darn near hopeless against a pair of queens. To Texans, that might sound like the kind of advice you should be given in kindergarten, but most Northern players stumble upon hold 'em after playing seven-stud. To them, there are apparent similarities. Both games let you choose your best hand from among seven cards.

Since in seven-stud a pair of jacks has better than one chance in three of drawing out on a pair of queens, they feel the same should be true for hold 'em. It isn't. That's because hold 'em has five common cards. Both players use these cards. Much of the time that you improve your pair of jacks, your opponent will also improve his pair of kings. What if the flop is 10-10-10? All hold 'em players with any experience realize that this flop usually helps *only* the higher starting hand. The exception is if the weaker hand includes the final ten. Hold 'em players can't remember their first reaction upon seeing a flop like 10-10-10. The very first time it happened, they probably thought, "Oh, glory, three tens and two fours make a full house!" I reckon their fingers were scratching their chips before they figured out that the flop wasn't really much good.

Just to keep this trend of thought rolling, consider what happens when a beginning player has a pair of queens. Now the flop comes 10-10-10. He's apt to feel unbeatable. Not until fifth street turns up a king or an ace does it dawn on him that he isn't that safe after all.

Texans try to corral new hold 'em players all the time. We remember to tell friends all the subtle moves about when to fear a flush and which hands to raise after the flop. But we forget to give them the most obvious advice—the most helpful thing a pure beginner can learn about hold 'em.

That advice is: You're about to play a game different from

any kind of poker you've ever seen before. Your hand will consist of *only* two cards. After that, five cards will be turned up, which will belong to *everyone*. If those five cards help your hand, don't get too happy. They must help your hand *exclusively.*

32 When You Play Tight, It's Your Secret

They call them "rocks" and they come in all shapes and sizes. A rock is a player who waits and waits and finally comes out swinging with a poker hand so powerful that it's a big favorite against almost all comers.

A lot of good poker players started out as rocks. They abandoned that style of play when it became obvious that there was more money to be made with a selective but aggressive strategy. Aggressive poker puts fear in your opponents, it wins the chips, and it feeds your competitive instincts like nothing else.

Now, Quincy, he was one heck of a rock. You should have seen him the day he set foot in Vegas with $15,000 in his pockets. Well, he got into the biggest game going at the Dunes and the boys just ate him up. Of course, he was playing on a short bankroll, so you could probably forgive him for being a little less than reckless with his capital.

There's nothing wrong with being a rock, especially while you're building a bankroll. Trouble is, rocks get broke in the big poker games about as fast as high-stakes keno players. That's because there's something about a rock that tends to irritate accomplished players. Guys like Bobby Baldwin and Johnny Moss will really study a rock; they'll gauge his temperament, weigh his weaknesses and then, just when the man makes a move, they'll destroy him with an all-in bet that's bigger than his determination to call.

Sure, rocks start with good hands, but they seldom have the courage to follow through, and world-class players take advantage of this fact all the time.

So, anyway, here is young Quincy, a studious-looking lad with thin-rimmed glasses, sitting in our no-limit hold 'em for the first time. About twenty minutes after he sits down, he finally decides to play a hand. The blinds are $25/$25/$50 and he brings it in for $100. Everyone passes to me and I'm sitting on the $50 blind with A-10 of diamonds. The flop comes J-4-2. Now I've got the nut flush, and I bet $400. Quincy calls and raises a thousand. I toy with the idea of just calling and moving him all-in on the next card, but I figure (wrongly) that I better make my move now. I push $12,000 more into the pot— just about enough to tap him off should he make the call.

Well, this kid turns purple! My lord, I swear he's stopped breathing! Then he gulps down short breaths and just keeps staring at the pot. Now he starts to reason aloud. "Okay, I made it $100 before the flop and you called. Flop three diamonds. You bet $400, I made it $400 and . . . How much is your raise, Doyle?"

The dealer counts my chips and answers for me. "Twelve thousand, three hundred."

"Yeah, well, I pass," says Quincy. And at this point he turned his hole card upon the table. It's the K-Q. There was only one way he could have been beat. I had to have two diamonds including the ace. Well, that's what he figured I had, and it was a really good lay down.

But Quincy had made a terrible mistake, especially against opponents at that level of play. He had shown the hand. First of all, he really was playing a rocky game. He was short on money and inwardly afraid. Now there's nothing wrong with putting yourself under pressure or being inwardly afraid, but one thing's for sure: You do not want your opponents to know it! When you must play like a rock, try to keep it secret.

What did he expect to gain by showing his hand? I figure it was recognition. Naturally, I refused him the one thing he was seeking. I threw my A-10 away, and he never knew for sure whether or not he'd made a good laydown.

It took two more hours for the boys to latch onto the last of his bankroll, but they did it. It's a shame too, because Quincy had a lot of talent. In a big no-limit game against tough opponents, you should never show a quality laydown unless you intend to call in the future. When you're floundering around in the ocean, it's stupid to drop bait for the sharks.

33 Staying in Action

"I raise you back!" Ken slurred. Have you ever seen a pathetic looking hobo stumble off a freight train? That's about the best way to picture Ken.

Every few minutes he would walk out of the cardroom and into the adjoining tavern to gulp down another White Russian. On the last trip, his belligerent manner led to a minor scuffle with another drunk. Now his shirt was torn in several places. His eyes were blurred, his tie askew, and there was liquor slopped all over his suit and trousers.

And to think, only two hours ago, Ken had entered this poker room in Sweetwater, Texas perfectly sober and looking like the respectable businessman he was during the weekdays.

Every Saturday afternoon, the locals held a $5 limit seven-stud game. Ken always got drunk and went home broke. In the two months I'd been attending, there had been no exception.

Already, at age eighteen, I was a semi-skilled poker player. Because the competition in this game wasn't very tough (consisting mostly of businessmen and college kids), I'd managed to win every week so far.

Presently, I had to decide whether to raise Ken once more. After all, he'd done nothing but unload money today. I'd guess he was losing $500 at the time. More importantly, he flashed a wad of bills in the range of $2,000 and I was convinced that, before the day was over, he would lose all of it. Two weak players had already busted out today and three had quit winners.

Just three of us remained. It seemed inevitable that a kid named Percy and I would end up with Ken's money.

It was an exciting prospect, since I spent myself down to $100 and used that to buy into the game. Right now I had close to $200 in front of me.

Our hands were . . .

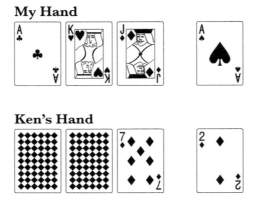

My Hand

Ken's Hand

"What do you do?" he prodded.

His demeanor was irritating, and I was tempted to raise and just keep raising. He probably didn't even have a pair, I figured. But I decided to exercise caution. After all, I didn't have a large enough bankroll that I could afford a big beat if he did have a concealed three of a kind. So I grabbed a $5 chip and started to call.

"Wait, son! Don't lose your courage. I'll show you my hand." Unbelievably, he turned over his hole card—Q-8.

You can't imagine the relief that flowed through my body. Knowing that my pair of aces was a small but clear favorite against his four-card flush, I shrugged my shoulders and raised.

"I raise," he responded.

So I raised again, scarcely believing my good fortune.

He raised! So I raised, and he raised, and I raised. By the time we reached the thirty-sixth raise and all my chips were in the pot, my head was spinning with excitement.

Only when Percy began to deal our next cards, did I recognize that I was still in jeopardy. Sure, I was the favorite, but Ken had a 47% chance of making a flush. During our raising war, I felt like I was in poker heaven. I just couldn't sling chips in fast enough. More than anything else, the knowledge that I had the edge and Ken was too dumb to realize it made me feel smug—yeah, smug is the right word. I guess I would've raised forever if my chips hadn't run out.

Alas, on the sixth card Ken caught a diamond. I ended up with the same two aces I'd started with.

Feeling cheated by fate, I slouched in my chair and watched in pitiful silence as Percy beat Ken out of $2,000.

Afterward, Percy said, "You should never have kept raising against his diamonds."

"What are you talking about?" I stormed, in no mood to take advice, particularly from a player with over two grand in his pocket while I didn't even have a buck for a hamburger.

"I guess you think a four-flush is supposed to beat a pair of aces," I grumbled sarcastically.

Percy said simply, "You risked everything when you were just a small favorite to get his money. Why do that? When someone plays as bad as Ken does, you should wait 'til you're certain to get his chips. Why settle for a little edge if a big edge is available?"

He left me alone, broke and miserable with nothing to do except think about it.

PART VII:

Home Poker

*"There's no place like home—
except a public poker room."*

# 34 *Rules for Home Poker*

You just wouldn't believe some of the arguments I've seen sprout up in so-called "friendly" poker games.

Probably the craziest one of all was at this dollar-limit game when I was nineteen years old, maybe twenty.

It started when a cranky old Californian named Frank growled, "You didn't ante!"

"I sure did!" objected Baker, a kid my age who nobody ever called by his first name.

"Look, Baker, you didn't ante! You can't play that hand unless you ante," Frank persisted.

Well, the quarrel got loud, real loud, and before anyone knew what was happening, old Frank picked up a coke bottle and hurled it. He explained later that he was just throwing it against the wall to show Baker he meant business.

The bottle struck Baker high on the forehead. He tilted back and slumped off his chair. We gathered around him and, for a moment, we thought he was dead.

We were in a basement. The kid who was banking the game ran upstairs to get his brother, a pre-med student.

The brother seemed at a loss. "Could be a concussion," he said, feeling Baker's scalp. "Maybe not. Hard to tell with head wounds." This guy was going to make a hell of a doctor.

Luckily, Baker groaned and started to come around. The

future doctor asked, "What happened, anyway?" Three of us spoke at once: "He forgot to ante!"

This is my conception of how a home poker game should be handled. If it settles any arguments or keeps anyone from being bopped in the head with a coke bottle, then I figure this chapter was worth writing.

In earlier articles, I talked about two of the very important disputes that come up over and over in poker games.

One is sandbagging, which is when you check a powerful hand (or possibly even a bluffing hand), get an opponent to bet and then raise. Some folks think that's bad manners, but I say it's good poker. If you all agree not to allow sandbagging in your game, fine. That's the rule you'll have to abide by. But if sandbagging is allowed, or more commonly, if nothing has been mentioned one way or the other, then check-raising is a powerful weapon that should be used whenever it's profitable.

The second thing that causes a lot of disputes is whether you should bluff your friends. Yes, and there can be no compromise here. When you're in a poker game, *everyone* is the enemy. You should play your friends just as hard as anyone else. Once that's understood, there won't be any hurt feelings.

Here are some other answers to recurring home game questions:

Can a player call for just the amount that's in front of him or does he have to match a bet to win a hand?

Not only *can* a player call for just the amount of chips or money he has remaining on the table, he should not be allowed to bet or call in excess of this. The practice of going into your wallet to cover a bet has no place in any poker game, public or private.

You should play only the chips on the table, always.

Must you "burn" a card before dealing?

The most important thing is that you stick to whatever the rule is. Dealer's choice is a common form of home poker. In it, the dealer can select what kind of poker game he wants to deal (i.e., seven-stud, five-draw, etc.), but should never have a *choice* about whether or not to burn a card.

Don't games like high-low split—where players declare in turn—and five-card draw, give the dealer a strong positional advantage?

Yes, and that's why it's better to have each player choose a game and then play it for a full round, rather than just one hand.

Who settles disputes?

Before the game begins, players should decide on a final arbiter whose judgment cannot be contested. However, should this player be involved in the pot, a vote of the inactive players must be taken.

When should the game adjourn?

Always at an exact predetermined time. This is especially important in home games to avoid hard feelings among losers who want the game to continue.

What would be an acceptable excuse for leaving a private game early, especially if you're a big winner?

You never need an excuse to leave a poker game. The notion that you can't quit a winner is just plain silly. If you think you're outclassed, you should quit. If you're tired, quit. If you're feeling unsure about the honesty of a player in the game, quit. But most of all, if you feel like taking your winnings home and spending them in the morning, quit.

It should be expressly understood that any poker player has

the unquestionable right to quit a game at any time, without being ridiculed.

In five-card draw poker, what's the maximum number of cards a player should be allowed to draw, three or four?
Five.

If you announce a bet but don't put your chips in, is your verbal action binding?
It depends on the game. If there's no agreement, you probably can't force a player to put his money in the pot. Almost all world-class players will honor their stated bets or calls whether the rules require them to do so or not. They do this as a matter of honor.

Is the host expected to extend credit to the players he's invited?
No. Not unless arrangements have been made in advance.

If you lend money to one player in a "friendly" game, are you morally obligated to lend to others?
No.

If, when cashing out at game's end, there are more chips than money to cover them, who's responsible?
The host or whoever has agreed to take on the responsibilities of the "banker." One player should be selected before the game starts to sell chips and buy them back. Balancing these transactions is his obligation.

Is it legal to have a private home-poker game?
In most parts of the United States it's a crime. Keep the drapes closed.

35 A Home Poker Dilemma

Before you decide to host that friendly weekly poker game, there are some things you ought to keep in mind.

First, what do you suppose is the most critical problem you're going to deal with? Now, if you think it's whether or not to reraise with a full house, you'd better figure it through again!

You might have headaches that have nothing to do with how much to bet or how many cards to draw. In fact, when you organize a private poker game and hold it at your house, these will be a few of your concerns:

1. Making certain that enough players actually show up for the game.

2. Establishing the rules and avoiding misunderstandings.

3. Setting betting limits that seem reasonable to those you've invited.

In future chapters, I'll talk about these things in detail and about establishing successful home games in general. Right now I want to discuss lending money, because that's far and away the ugliest problem you'll be up against.

There's just no getting around it; if you're going to host a poker game, players will ask to borrow money. It's all right to lend within reason, but you must establish a rigid policy and stick to it. Failure to do so can be fatal to your game. Too much lending can develop into what I call "Dean's Disease."

Dean was a bright college kid with rich parents and a seemingly endless supply of money. We were both in our junior year at Hardin-Simmons when I met him. Every Saturday afternoon, sometimes lasting deep into the night, Dean held a game at his parents' house.

He probably had the most liberal lending policy of any poker host I've ever known. The kid just never said no! I mean, I felt embarrassed about the way the others would take advantage of him. Typically, a guy would come to the game with $30 in his pocket. That would last about twenty minutes.

Then it was, "Dean, can you spare fifty 'til next week?"

Dean would hand over the chips from his stack or the cash from his wallet. He never even grumbled.

Once, after the game, I questioned his charity, "Aren't you going a little heavy on the lending?"

"Naw, these guys are good for it."

Once, two players showed up for the game without any money at all! Dean promptly gave them $50 each to buy in. "Don't worry," he told them as he placed their chips on the table, "I know you guys are good for it."

He was half right. One of them paid, but the other guy has never been seen since. One day Dean showed me a notebook in which he'd listed all the money he was owed from this poker gathering. It totaled $2,670—mostly from players who had quit the game months ago.

Next Saturday he gave $200 to a newcomer none of us had ever played with before. "I'd be a little worried," I told him privately. "That guy just never has any money, and he owes a lot around campus already."

"I'll lay you three to one he's good for it," was Dean's response. I remember saying, "Three to one isn't good enough!" And that's the point. Think about this: If you lend out $100 four times and get repaid three times, you've lost $100 of a total $400 loaned. That's 25%. If you're into big gambling, lending $10,000 at a crack, it costs you $2,500 per loan, even though you think a man is three to one to repay it! Now who in their right mind would fork over $10,000 only to get $7,500 back on average?

Well, poker players lend smaller sums on that basis all the time! When you have a home poker game, liberal lending policies are especially dangerous. First, even if you're a winning player, you'll probably lose more on bad loans than you win at the table. Second, players who get in over their heads will invariably take one course of action: they'll stop coming to the game!

Just remember: Dean's Disease kills poker games!

36 Getting More Chips than You Bargained For

I was the last one to cash out.

"How much you got there, Doyle?" Tripper was smiling because his Wednesday night game had been successful. Everyone had shown up and he'd won close to $100, pretty big stuff because all of us were just working kids.

I puzzled over the amount of cash that remained on the table. Something was wrong! He had already paid off five players, and he and I only had chips that remained to be counted. In front of Tripper was exactly $115 worth of chips. He'd played all night on a $20 buy-in. On the table there was $160 in cash: seven $20 bills and four $5 bills.

"Did you count your chips? How much do you have?" Tripper prompted. "Ninety-two dollars," I said solemnly, knowing these weren't the words he was hoping to hear.

"Huh? Ninety-what? Let me count 'em."

Everyone else had just left, so while he counted down my stacks there was silence except for the clicking together of the plastic chips. Having counted, he sighed. He stood up and paced to within six inches of a wall, pivoted and came back toward me. He stumbled on the carpet and fell, amazingly, right back into his chair. (You don't earn a name like Tripper for nothing!)

It was my turn to probe. "Well, how much was it?"

"You're right . . . Here, take it!" He scooped up four

twenties and three fives and hurled them at me. What this gesture lacked was conviction, because those bills floated and spun daintily back to the table.

"I owe you $3," I said, and handed over three singles from my pocket.

He put these beside the money that remained on the poker table. Now there was only $68: three twenties, a five and three ones. Take away the $20 Tripper had originally invested and his profit was $48, which was about half of what he'd expected.

Calming down somewhat, he complained, "You saw me count the chips. I was sure everyone got the right amount. I double-checked everything."

While he grumbled, he began jamming the chips into a revolving rack that held them. He filled up one column, then the next. This experience was so upsetting to him that he didn't even follow his normal post-game procedure of organizing the chips according to color.

"How could I have counted wrong, Doyle?" he demanded.

"Well, I reckon you made some mistake . . . or . . ." I watched him stuffing the last column full of chips. "Or . . ."

"I don't understand," he moaned as the rack overflowed and extra chips spilled to the tabletop.

"It's pretty simple, Tripper. Somebody brought in some spare chips."

Well, we never did find out who'd done this evil deed. But it's a more common occurrence than you might figure. I've heard of two other games where unscrupulous players padded their wallets by sneaking additional chips onto the table.

That's the problem with cheap plastic chips. All a thief needs to do is shop around. Usually he can find the same brand that the poker host is using. After that, it's just a matter of how much he wants to steal.

So what's my advice? Use money? No. Few things inhibit the pace of a poker game so much as using hard currency.

With chips, players tend to be less aware of how much they're betting. Maybe they maintain a dollar amount in their mind, but it doesn't mean the same as betting with bills that are spendable.

I've seen a few no-limit games where they used cash. Believe me, this tends to be a bluffer's paradise! You swing with a $5,000 bet and an opponent must call with fifty hundred-dollar bills. He's apt to think, "Holy cow! This will cost four video recorders and a trip to Mexico City!" So he probably won't call.

But when you're using chips, they're "just chips" and the pace of the game is far more liberal.

The fact that you can bluff more successfully is about the only important reason to favor cash over chips. By and large, most experts agree that a poker game flows better when chips are used. So what's the alternative to inexpensive plastic chips? Buy a specially made set with your initials on them, registered by a reputable company. They will guarantee that the design is reserved for your chips only, so no duplicates will be sold to anyone else. It's a little expensive, but it's worth the money. You shouldn't even consider having a home game without professional-quality chips.

Of course, even quality chips can be dangerous. One friend complained that his books didn't balance following a high-limit game. Someone had pocketed chips on a night that the limit was small and cashed them in when the chips were given a greater value. This is easy to do since personalized poker chips rarely have any value stamped on them. The host decides night-to-night which color has what value.

So, if you're going to host a "friendly" game, you'd better have ethical friends.

Cardoza Publishing   165

37 A Smooth Game and Nobody Came

Do you know what a "smooth" poker game is? Well, I didn't either 'til I met up with Diamond Herb. Nobody could ever figure out where he got his nickname, since he never wore jewelry. Whenever he wasn't around, we liked to call him Smooth Herb.

There's probably nothing that will mess up a friendly home game as quick as a law-and-order card player. You know the type. They would rather decide a pot on some silly technicality than on the obvious merits of each hand. This was Smooth Herb.

Sure, we all acknowledge the need for rules, especially at home games where disputes jump up and burn you out of nowhere. But guys like Smooth Herb take all the pleasure out of poker.

Now this was back in 1962 at a medium-sized pot-limit hold 'em game that went off every Friday night in San Antonio. The regular players on the Texas circuit liked this game because the host, Ken, had a really comfortable layout. Ken was about seventy, and soft-spoken, with a really active mind. Most of the players in this game were in their twenties or early thirties, so Ken naturally became sort of a father figure for us.

This was the first time any of us had ever played poker against Smooth Herb. As we were plopping down in the super-soft chairs around the poker table, he shouted, "Wait!"

We all looked at him curiously. Wait for what? Let's play poker. "How do you know who gets which seats?" he demanded.

"Son, you just take any seat that pleases you," Ken smiled.

"That isn't the right way to do it. You should cut cards for seats."

"Why?" I asked.

"Because, Doyle, that's what makes a smooth game. If a game is smooth, it pays in the long run."

Everyone thought this was rude of the newcomer, and a few of us grumbled about how this game had run fine for over a year without cutting for seats. But Ken said, "Let's show our new guest a little courtesy."

So we cut for seats and that made Smooth Herb seem happy. He won the first few pots and then a player named Paul called a bet and raised $100.

"Are you calling me or raising me?" Herb wanted to know.

Ken interrupted, "The man said he was raising, son."

"I know what he said," Herb countered, "but his chips aren't all the way in the pot."

"Sure they are," Ken explained. "There's the chips Paul called with, and there's another hundred on the table in front of him. That's a raise." But Smooth Herb insisted, "Maybe we should draw us a circle 'round the pot, so we know when a bet gets made."

Now there came a slight irritation in Ken's voice. His soft elderly drawl cracked as he said, "Son, we never had much trouble before, figuring out who raised and who didn't."

Finally, Herb muttered to himself and yielded. He made the call and lost the pot. By evening's end, he was roughly even. During the six hours of play he had complained often about rules that needed clarification. Here was a true stickler for detail.

The next time he attended the game, a player said, "Go ahead."

"You can say 'check' or you can say 'pass.'" Smooth Herb corrected. "If you say anything else, that doesn't make it legal."

This time there was a really big argument with me and all the other players taking the side that it didn't matter what words a man used, as long as he was honorable and we understood what he meant.

Finally, the man who had originally barked, "go ahead" lost his patience. He couldn't decide whether to punch Herb out or just give in. At last he shrugged his shoulders and said, "Ah, what's the difference. I pass."

Over the next few weeks Herb kept complaining about the game not being smooth. There was some talk about not letting him play anymore. But all in all, he wasn't a bad sort of person away from the table, so we just sort of tolerated his behavior.

Then the host, Ken, took sick and we either had to cross San Antonio off the circuit or find another local place to play. As luck would have it, Smooth Herb was the only one with a house around San Antonio.

We scheduled the game. I showed up a few minutes early to find myself alone with Herb.

"A couple of the guys called and said they couldn't make it," he explained. "The rest will be coming along pretty soon . . . I guess." Nobody came. I don't guess any of them stayed away just to be ornery. In the back of their minds they had this idea that playing at Smooth Herb's would be an unpleasant experience, so they found other things to do. Ken recovered, but that marked the end of the game in San Antonio.

The point is that rules should grow out of necessity and nothing else. If your home game runs harmoniously without a lot of definitions, then you should leave it alone.

There's an aftermath to this story. Two years ago I was

playing at the Dunes in a game with Bobby Baldwin. I'd told Bobby about Smooth Herb many times, but I think he figured I was exaggerating. Suddenly I saw Herb coming into the card room. It had been a lot of years but we still recognized each other. He said hello warmly, and I introduced him to Bobby. Then Herb watched the game from a distance, electing not to play.

A few hours later, Bobby cashed in, winning $40,000. Shortly after, Smooth Herb came up to where Bobby and I were standing and complained, "That might be a good game, but it scares me. It doesn't look very smooth."

Bobby, who is one of the true gentlemen of poker, smiled softly, "That's true. It isn't smooth, but you can still spend it."

# 38 *Home Games Need Leaders*

Deciding on the rules and regulations that govern your home poker game can be a little like a group of six-year-olds arguing the rules of Monopoly. Everyone has his own vague understanding of the way things ought to be. And, sadly, no two people think the same way.

In the past, I've stressed how important it is to set down the rules *before* you play poker. In the heat of a Texas-sized pot with the grocery money at stake—well, that's no time to decide whether or not it's legal to sandbag.

Before the very first hand is dealt in a new poker game, someone should lay down the rules. I think, in the beginning, one man should decide. Many times I've seen grown men— trying to be fair—argue for hours. Democracy is fine, but in the beginning someone should lead the troops.

I'll tell you a little story about a game we tried to start back in college. In my junior year, this sophomore, Carl, and I used to play heads-up a lot off campus. The only game we ever played was hold 'em and the stakes were mighty small by what we're used to today. Sometimes we'd play hours-long freeze-outs for as little as $20.

Anyway, we had several other friends who'd expressed a casual interest in poker. At Carl's urging they gathered in his parent's basement one Saturday afternoon for our first group game.

"Let's get started," nagged Danny, a freshman.

"First we need to agree on some conditions," Carl insisted. "Everyone sit down at the table."

Eventually, using his fist like a gavel, Carl brought the meeting to order. He took a long list of things to be decided from his shirt pocket. He wondered, "First, what kind of stakes do you want to play for?"

Dollar-limit with a quarter ante was decided, but deciding ate up ten minutes because everyone wanted his say.

Next Carl wanted to know, "What's the limit on raises?"

One kid, whose name I don't even remember, became really adamant about why there shouldn't be a limit on raises. Another kid wanted four raises, arguing that three were obviously not enough and five were too many. He devised a long argument about how you get trapped with the fifth raise, but how the ability to raise four times was a necessary strategic option "in a good poker game."

Then Carl put several minor points to a vote.

Next he opened the discussion to wild-card games. That brought a tornado of chaos. Well, you just never saw anything like it. Two guys were insisting that you should never have more than four wild cards, one man wanted no wild cards at all and several thought that the dealer should decide whatever he wanted.

Then there was Danny, who kept saying, "Come on, let's deal." Well, the argument over wild cards just went on and on. Finally, Carl insisted on a vote. Dealer's choice won. The guy who had debated loudly against any wild cards stormed out, declaring he wasn't going to play any "sissy game."

A friend left with him, because he didn't have transportation of his own. Someone else said, "I don't guess I wanna play five-handed. Five-handed isn't poker."

So he left and then someone else left.

Danny played three-handed with Carl and me for about

ten minutes. Then he excused himself. That left us to play our normal heads-up freeze out. So it goes . . .

I think it's all right to let the players influence the rules, but on that first game someone should appoint himself leader, set down the rules, shuffle and deal.

39 Unfriendly Stakes

They tell you old friends make the best poker pals. Well, whoever said that first couldn't crawl his way through a dust storm in the Panhandle. I mean, there's just nobody I hate to play with more than a group of giddy gooses, all liquored up and discussing old times around some poker table in the basement.

Unfortunately, that's the only kind of poker a lot of folks ever get to play. If you live in Longmont, Colorado, for example, you can't go advertising for new players in the local paper. Often these games end up with a whole gathering of uncles and aunts and some brother-in-law who's visiting the neighbor up the street.

A lot of friendly games are just casual contests among old pals who struggled through college together. There's a similarity, I think, between such games and the bridge parties for neighborhood housewives. Poker games of this sort tend to be loose and informal. Rules are rules, but the boys seem to piece them together whenever it seems necessary, rather than thinking them out in advance.

And that, brother, brings me to my main objective about too-friendly poker games. Maybe your idea of a good time is sitting down with Oscar Madison and the boys, but I've seen a lot of good men lose a lot of money under those circumstances.

Usually these games start off small. But week after week (or sometimes hour after hour), the taste for higher-stakes poker beckons. Pretty soon a game that started off $1 limit is $20 dollar limit with all sorts of wild cards thrown in, and George is writing Norman a check for twenty-five hundred bucks. It begins to hurt. Things get serious fast.

Let me tell you, there's just nothing that will cool down a friendship as quickly as one buddy going out to buy new carpet with the money that was supposed to go toward purchasing the loser's vacation property on the lake.

When the stakes increase, those gentlemen's agreements about making up the rules as you go along suddenly seem dangerous.

There are plenty of arguments at these "friendly" games. Two years ago, I was invited to a friend's for dinner. There was a poker party downstairs. Some of my good pals from college were seated comfortably around an old dining room table. At first, there was a maximum $5 bet. Four hours later it was pot-limit with a $10 blind. If you know much about pot-limit, you'll recognize that this can get mighty expensive.

My friend Alex, who sort of got roped into the game to begin with, was losing $1,500. His wife came downstairs.

"How much?" she screamed upon learning of her husband's disaster. "I'll win it back. Just sit there and be calm," he instructed.

But she would have none of it. "Let's just say goodbye to these nice people and head on home." Her voice was heavy with sarcasm. So Alex left like a dog trying to hide his tail. Luckily I hadn't agreed to play, because two very vocal arguments popped up on the following hands. One was about whether Paul had the right to grab his hand back out of the discards.

Well, this pot was around $1,200, and everyone was serious about Paul having a dead hand.

"But the same thing happened to Alex the first hand we played tonight. And we all let him play the hand," Paul protested.

The host said, "Yeah, but we were only playing for five bucks then." And that settled the argument.

Here's a little advice: Decide in advance whether the kind of poker you're going to play is social or serious. If it's social, play for painless stakes and make up the rules as you go. But if it's serious, define the rules, forget your friendships and play to win.

40 Sticking with the Rules

"String bet! String bet!" cried big Ed as I raised. There were only two players competing for this seven-stud pot—Kenny, a quiet kid with no knack for poker, and me. It was fourth street and Kenny had wagered the $10 limit.

I had A-K in the hole and A-Q showing. Kenny showed 4-A on the board. My only worry was that he might have 4-4 or A-4 hidden. Clearly this was a raising situation. Ed's almost hostile complaint stunned the group at our weekly game in Amarillo. There was momentary silence.

"You're not even in the pot!" one of the players finally shot at Ed.

"You don't need to be in the pot to keep the rules straight," Ed defended. "I say it's a string bet and that's that. Doyle called, and then he went back to his chips to raise. If that ain't what a string bet is, then I must be dreaming!"

Now Kenny himself came to my defense. "Well, you must be dreaming, then, 'cause Doyle didn't do anything wrong. He said, 'Raise' before he went back to his chips. So if you don't mind, just sit back and let us play the pot out."

I smiled faintly and the other players nodded their agreement. You'd think that would be the end of it, but it wasn't. Ed stood up, his giant frame adding to the intimidation of his coming words. He growled, "No, I ain't going to sit back and let you play the pot! Maybe you heard Doyle say 'Raise' and maybe you didn't. It doesn't make one bit of difference because I didn't hear it. Maybe I'm not in this pot, but my chips are still on the table and I intend to ante next hand, so I guess my say is as good as anybody else's!"

Several in the group shook their heads disbelievingly. I just smiled and tried to be gracious. I always figure a man shouldn't get bent out of shape over a simple poker quarrel. Obviously, my raise was perfectly proper and should have been allowed, but whether that extra ten dollars stayed in the pot or returned to my stack was not a life-or-death matter.

Unfortunately, the other players took it more seriously. Some were genuinely peeved at Ed, and the more they attacked him, the more defensive he became. He clenched his teeth and grimaced. I grinned. Kenny seemed bewildered. Three players snarled back at the standing man. Clearly this friendly game had taken a brief turn toward the battlefield.

Finally, five of the players verbally argued Ed into a near silence. He slammed himself back into his chair, still grumbling to himself. The raise was allowed.

Almost apologetically, Kenny reraised immediately! I passed and he showed me that, sure enough, he'd been rolled up with three fours. Except for the fact that Ed tried to assert himself several times during the remainder of the session by finding rule violations wherever he could invent them, the game went smoothly, but it simply wasn't fun.

Well, I'm a firm believer that home poker players should decide what the rules are in advance. But home poker should never become a court of law. You've got to make reasonable decisions based on the facts at hand. Within limits, flexibility makes a game flow.

The three things you should bring to a poker game are your brains, your bankroll and some good manners.

PART VIII:
More Winning Wisdom

"They say: 'It's not whether you win or lose, it's how you play the game.' They're wrong!"

41 Letting the Dog Die

We were playing deuce-to-seven in Sam's basement. I guess most Northerners don't know how to play Kansas City—which is another name for the game. To me, it's the most skillful form of lowball poker. From Austin to Topeka, from Amarillo to Joplin, you just didn't play lowball any other way in the late sixties.

Deuce-to-seven is an almost perfect no-limit game. (I'll give you the rules and some hints later.) A man's fortune can turn inside out so quick you think you're watching *The Twilight Zone.* Since it's a variation of five-card draw, you often don't have any clues about how strong your opponent is. He can slide $10,000 into a lowly $200 pot and suddenly you've got to decide whether his hand is perfect or perfectly awful.

Well, back when I was traveling through Texas and nearby states, scurrying from poker game to poker game, there was a lot of big-limit deuce-to-seven. Sam's game, though, was medium-limit and you hardly ever heard of anyone winning or losing more than $2,000.

Although everyone I hung around with occasionally attended his Thursday or Saturday night game, most of us tried to avoid it whenever there was something else going on.

The one thing that annoyed us about Sam was his habit of quitting whenever he had a big score. Now, I believe that a man should never need an excuse to quit a poker game, but it was the way Sam went about it that was bothersome. You see, he was the host; it was *his* game. Usually, the host doesn't quit early just because he's a big winner. Maybe that's bad manners and maybe it isn't.

What irritated me about Sam was that he thought he needed an excuse to quit. And, brother, did he come up with some good ones! Once he feigned an ulcer attack that would have been more convincing had he grasped his stomach instead of his head during all the moaning and groaning. He cashed out his $1,800 winnings and sent everyone home. One night, leading by $2,100, he leaned back in his chair, stretched an arm above his head and awkwardly banged a water pipe with his beer can.

"What the heck are you doing?" quizzed one of the players. "Nothing. Just an accident."

Well, it sure was a strange-looking accident. I wasn't surprised at all when, within a minute of his clanging on the pipe, Sam's wife came charging down the stairs crying, "Honey, honey, something terrible just happened!"

She wore a faded robe and her hair was in curlers. We'd seen her looking better. "What's the problem?" Sam wanted to know. Some of the rest of us glanced at each other. We knew what was coming. Sam was about to excuse himself from the game again. Linda said, "It's Ruffian. He ate a hot dog someone left on the porch and he looks sick. I think he's been poisoned."

So Sam explained how his dog Ruffian was like a child to him. "This'll be my last hand, gentlemen." Turning to Linda, he added, "Don't worry, baby, we'll just have to wake up the vet. Ruffian's going to pull through." Then he winked at her secretly, but we all saw it.

Now this next hand came down like it was something out of a poor movie script. I looked and found myself holding 7-5-4-3-2. That's the best possible hand, and the chances against getting it pat are more than 2,500 to 1. Everyone folded and Sam called my $15 blind and raised $40. I figured I shouldn't push him too far before the draw, so I raised it back a hundred. He called promptly.

After I stood pat, he drew one. I debated whether to bet small and hope to get raised or bet everything and pray he'd make enough to call. Then I thought, maybe I can figure some way to really lay it on him. So I checked.

"A thousand," Sam announced. That was an unusually big bet because the pot was scarcely over $300. I raised everything that remained in front of him, slightly less than $2,000. Luckily, he had the second best possible hand, 7-6-4-3-2, and he called.

"Poor baby!" soothed his wife, wrapping an arm around his shoulder as I raked in the biggest pot Sam's game had ever seen. "Come on, we better look after Ruffian." Now *she* winked at him, a wink that indicated she was insensitive to his pain.

"Not now!" Sam hissed, and he extracted $500 from his wallet, trembling. "Sell me some of them chips, Doyle."

Linda didn't quite grasp what was happening. Obviously she'd been told to come rushing downstairs when he banged on the pipe. So she began babbling, "Do you want me to go back upstairs?" Then, to give more impact to her story, so that the others wouldn't get wise to the lie, she added, "Do you want me to take Ruffian to Dr. Fryman?"

At this point Sam broke under the strain. His healthy win had turned into a nightmare on a single hand and this woman kept tugging at his shoulder, unaware of his agony.

Finally he shoved her away, not very gently, and screamed, "Look, Linda, get out of here and let the dog die!"

Well, word got around Texas about that episode, and pretty soon, whenever a man had to leave a game, someone would spout, "Don't quit now. Just let the dog die." Maybe you remember hearing that expression. Now you know how it started.

Deuce-to-seven (Kansas City lowball) is almost the exact opposite of conventional poker. You can just imagine how it got started. It was probably some home game, dealer's choice, and some guy said, "I've got an idea. This time let's play the worst hand wins!" So they tried it and liked it.

That's about all there is to know about it. You get five cards and you can draw as many as you want. Normally, what's the worst possible poker hand?

You're looking at it. In deuce-to-seven, this is the best hand. Unlike ace-to-five lowball, straights and flushes are not ignored. They almost always lose in a showdown. That's why a one-card draw to 7-6-5-4 is not very good. If you catch an 8 or a 3, you've got no way to win except by bluffing. Contrast that one-card draw to 7-6-5-2. Providing those are not all the same suit, that's a very strong draw because you can't make a straight or a flush by accident.

The same is true of two-card draws. Any two-card draw should include *both* a deuce and a seven: 7-5-2 is good, 7-5-3 is bad. There's only one other rule you need to know. Aces are *always* high. Therefore, 5-4-3-2-A is not a straight; it's an ace-high hand. I suggest you play no-limit. But be prepared for a lot of swings. Your bankroll will do a lot of hopping around, and sometimes you'll feel like your dog died.

42 Thanks for the Pleasure Players

I don't like the word "sucker." As Bobby Baldwin pointed out in *Bobby Baldwin's Winning Poker Secrets*, not everyone plays poker for the same reason. Maybe you're in it to make money and maybe you're not.

Some folks will consider it almost sinful to talk about playing poker for recreation, but millions of Americans do just that. I'd wager that for every single person who masters the game, several thousand are just casual players who take their breaks as they come, hoping to win a little extra spending money.

Well, there's nothing wrong with that! Professional football players don't go around chastising amateurs for throwing awkward passes at the city park. Lawyers don't ridicule laymen for misunderstanding legal terminology. Surgeons don't expect you to make your own incisions.

Poker is one of those rare endeavors in which amateurs and professionals meet on identical turf. There are seldom any handicaps given, and none are expected. As often as not, the weakest high-limit players are very successful in some other profession. Maybe I'm growing older and less tolerant, but sometimes it annoys me when a marginal poker pro barely earning his living begins to mock the play of an opponent. Quite often that opponent has spent many, many years mastering the complexities of his profession. Had he spent that same time unraveling the mysteries of poker, he may very well be world-class. But he didn't and he isn't.

What he is, often, is a highly paid master of his own game, earning ten times the income of the needling hustler. I've always felt blessed that non-professionals are attracted to poker. If this were not the case, there would be no professionals. The bottom line is, there can be no winners without losers. Don't ever let anyone say you must take poker seriously. But if you do choose to take it seriously, be grateful that there are enough successful folks out there that play for pleasure.

The reason weaker players are content to play against strong competition is that there is luck involved. Enough luck so that, even if a man finds himself outclassed, he still might end up buying a new television with a professional player's money. Skillful players often moan because there's too much luck involved in poker. They feel it gives those suckers too much of a chance.

But, first of all, those players wouldn't be there if it weren't for the luck factor. Just why would they play if they knew for sure they'd lose? And secondly, those are not suckers. Many times I've been at a poker table overflowing with doctors and lawyers and college professors. Some of them play well, some play badly, and some don't care. If you take poker seriously, then you ought to treat it like a business. But who says you have to take it seriously? Poker is great recreation.

"What an idiot!" a player once whispered to me, nodding to a doctor across the poker table. "He don't know enough to throw away a pair of sixes against an obvious flush."

Two hours later that same player suffered a chest pain and immediately sought the doctor's advice. Is this normal? How can you tell it's not a heart attack?

He wanted to know everything, and the doctor answered calmly and professionally. It turned out to be nothing, and here are some words the doctor never said: "You're an idiot. You can't even tell heartburn from a heart attack!" Too bad—those words would have been appropriate.

 **43** *Quitting While You're Ahead*

America's first Power Poker Seminar was held in November 1981. A week before, I talked to a dealer from one of the biggest poker rooms in Las Vegas. He pondered the $195 cost for the two-day course and shook his head. "Doyle, at that price you'll be lucky to get ten people."

"How come?" With poker wizards Mike Caro and David Sklansky teaching by my side, I figured we could ask $1,000 easy. "Don't get me wrong, it's worth the money, but there aren't enough players who realize it. Poker players think the game's mostly luck. They might pay $20 for a little advice, but they absolutely won't fork over $200 and spend two whole days away from their jobs."

So I explained how *Gambling Times*, the sponsor of the seminar, was already projecting an audience between forty and sixty.

"I'll have to see it to believe it," the dealer said. Then we made a friendly bet. He wagered there would be fewer than twenty-five paid. Well, brother, he lost bad!

On November 18, 1981, so many poker players showed up at the Rainbow Club in Gardena, California, that we were forty minutes late getting everyone registered. At final count, there were ninety-one paid. Thirty came from out of state, even though the advertised emphasis was on California-style draw poker.

Call this the dawn of something special. If there are any poker historians out there, they will want to include this seminar as the first positive evidence that poker had grown beyond its infancy.

You talk about folks taking poker seriously! Our audience was the most sophisticated I'd ever seen. They asked questions of David and Mike that were right on the money. I'm used to being interviewed by radio and TV personalities who want to know, "Should you draw to an inside straight?"

I was especially impressed by the way Mike and David fielded the more difficult theoretical questions. There simply aren't two other poker experts alive who understand this game in greater depth. I guess we all learned from each other.

When the seminar ended, few in the audience wanted to leave. I noticed a large group gathered around Mike, taking notes and asking questions. David, too, had his followers who were reluctant to let him go.

For me, the experience was rewarding. When I first began to play, there were no real authorities you could count on. It was the player with the most courage and the best intuition who prospered. Those things are still important, but the scientific age has come to poker.

The other day, I was drifting through a casino when this crabby middle-aged woman stormed past, clutching her poker-playing husband by the sleeve. "How come you didn't quit while you were eight hundred ahead?" she quarreled.

"Don't know," he mumbled.

"Well, it's pretty stupid winnin' $20 when we could've bought a new refrigerator. You're supposed to be such a smart poker player. How come you kept playin'?"

"Don't know"

If you've been around the poker tables much, you've probably heard that kind of talk before. There is no scientific way of determining when to quit. If you've got the best of a game, you might just as well play 'til you get tired of it. If that poor man won $2,000, his wife wouldn't have been asking why he hadn't quit when he was $800 up. Quit when you feel like quitting, that's my advice.

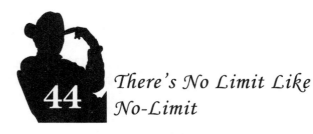

44 *There's No Limit Like No-Limit*

As you know, my favorite game, is no-limit hold 'em. Poker is a game of people, and nothing brings this fact out as clearly as a no-limit confrontation.

When you're playing limit poker—even a big-limit game like $200/$400—you never have to face the fear of a man jumping up from out of nowhere and moving all-in against you. You can bet $400 on the last card knowing that the very worst thing that can happen is you'll get raised another $400.

If you've got some middling hand when that raise comes, then you've got to make a decision about whether to call or fold. That decision, though, doesn't pack the same agony that arises in a no-limit situation when you bet $400 and suddenly are facing a $5,000 raise.

Even so, there are levels of no-limit games, and most folks don't take this into account. For instance, if you begin with very small antes and blinds—say a total of $1—then your no-limit game is going to be pretty small. After all, you have to make bets that seem reasonable when measured against how much money is in the pot. In a small game you might open for $1, get raised $3 and reraise $5. That would be a considerable amount of action, but still the pot would be a down-to-earth size.

Suppose the total blinds and antes added up to $1,000. Now your no-limit game has some size to it. You open for $1,000, get raised $3,000, and raise back $5,000. You're looking at a hold 'em pot that's up near $20,000 before the flop. The previous sum (when the blinds added up to just $1) was under $20. The action was the same in both games; the *amounts* were different.

Why is this discussion important? Well, a few weeks back, I saw this kid pass up a small no-limit game to sit in a $30 limit seven-stud game. His entire bankroll was $1,000. He lost it in about twenty minutes. As they were leaving the card room, his girlfriend tugged him by the sleeve and glanced over at the no-limit game. There must have been about $300 on the table, total, and everyone looked like they were having a good time.

"How come you didn't play in that game?" she asked.

"That's no-limit!" he grumbled. "I couldn't afford it."

Strangely, that's the attitude a lot of folks have, because the term "no-limit" carries a healthy wallop. A rational man should simply check the size of the blinds and the size of the antes (if any) and weigh that against the bulge in his wallet. No-limit is a type of poker, not a *size* of game.

 **45** *The Ploy's the Play*

Men are like little boys sometimes. Nothing proves this better than a poker game. I'll bet you've seen grown men sniveling, whining and throwing cards. You've seen them gloat in triumph. A poker table is an arena away from the real world. It is a field of combat and a place of escape.

The war of poker psychology is a real war with a lot at stake. People will do crazy things to win at poker.

About ten years back, I was playing in a home game and a studious-looking college kid named Tom pranced into the room eager to play. He was carrying two books, which he set on the edge of the poker table. One was something by John Steinbeck, and the other one we couldn't see.

Well, the game went along normally for a while. Then Jim, who was a cantankerous man growled, "What's that other book, boy?"

This was no-limit hold 'em, and suddenly Tom shoved $9,000 in bills and chips into a $700 pot. It was a good-sized poker game. We'd all seen bigger bets occasionally, but this one was really unexpected. I mean, you hardly ever saw Tom make anything but a reasonable bet. So now, Jim, who'd been about to throw his hand away, started to hesitate because this was so unusual. "My, my!" he said. "You sure you really got something?"

At this moment, Tom pushed Steinbeck off the other book

with his elbow. It looked like an accident, but it wasn't. The mystery book was black with the title screaming in fancy gold ink: *How to Bluff Constantly and Win!*

Sarcastically, Jim asked, "Did you learn much from that book, Tom?" Well, he just sat there sort of embarrassed and avoided Jim's eyes.

Now Jim delayed for a couple of minutes. Finally, dramatically, he rose from the table, shoved his stack in, and barked, "Count it down, son. There's about seven grand there, so I reckon you got change coming."

But Tom didn't even bother to take change. He merely flipped over his nut flush and raked in the pot.

You could see Jim struggling to find the right words. Finally, he grumbled a simple, "Goodnight, boys." He stormed out of there like a locomotive loose on the prairie.

Well, it was a good night for Tom. I've got to admit, every time he bet I had the urge to call. My professional discipline wouldn't let me yield to that urge, but I suspect some of the other players were not that disciplined. We were all mighty curious about the strange-titled book on the table, but Tom wouldn't let anyone read it. He guarded it against all assaults.

He cashed out finally—a big winner, seeming self-amused. As a parting gesture, he tossed the book into the center of the table and laughed, "Here, you guys need this more than I do."

About six grown-up men grabbed for the black book at once while Tom giggled like a kindergartner.

When we opened the book, *How to Bluff Constantly and Win*, there was nothing but blank pages. Except the first one, which contained the handwritten word, "Don't."

46 Fun With Even-Money Bets

Some men will sell their souls to get the best of a bet. I've seen a lot of friendships harpooned when someone forgot about fairness and tried to grab a few extra dollars by deception.

For some, hustling is both a lifelong addiction and an artistic endeavor. As much as I disdain hustling, there've been a few tilted wagers that stand out in my mind as truly creative.

One of them happened fifteen years ago in Dallas. Eddy and Foster were chums who would bet on anything. I once saw them make a hasty $200 bet on whether a runaway shopping cart would collide with a detour sign at the bottom of a hill. It did, and Eddy collected.

However, Eddy did not win most of the time. That's because Foster was one of those guys who always wanted a little extra edge. If a football line was seven points, he'd try for eight or nine. This led to friction, and once, while they were at our Friday night poker game, they got into an argument over it.

Finally, Eddy—who at twenty-three was young enough to be Foster's son—firmly announced that he wasn't "going to make no more bets 'til you start bein' square about it."

Well, after that, Foster did yield a mite. They'd bet on almost anything on TV while we played poker. A lot of times this was local stuff, sometimes high school football. They'd bet on game shows and on whether the newscast would break for a commercial within a ten-second period (they used a stopwatch).

With sports bets, they liked to negotiate, haggle about a fair settlement and pay off the bet before the game was over. Foster seemed more skilled at bargaining.

Then one night, a tennis match came on. Well, tennis wasn't big in Texas back then, but there was a chopped-up replay of an important match held earlier that day.

Now Foster says, "Let's bet on that."

And Eddy, he just grins and says, "No way. That there's a video tape replay."

So they fussed over it a little bit with Foster swearing he didn't know the outcome. Finally he came up with this idea: "This is supposed to be a dead-even match, so tell you what . . . You pick whichever guy you want for $500. Even if I know the winner already, even if I went to that there match in person, you can't possibly have the worst of it."

Eddy agreed that was so. It was my turn to deal cards. And while I slapped down the hold 'em hands, I watched Eddy fidget over his decision. Finally, he chose, "The guy with the long hair."

The bet was on. The first set went to Eddy's guy, no sweat. "How much you pay me to call it off?" Eddy cackled.

No response.

The next set went the same way and Eddy offered, "I'll let you out for four hundred." By this time Foster was winning about $400 at poker, and I figured maybe he'd jump at the chance to save $100 off his tennis misfortune.

"Fifty bucks," Foster countered.

"Fifty? You think I'm crazy. I done you a favor saying you could get out for four bills!"

Now the third and fourth sets went Foster's way. By now the long-haired player of Eddy's choice was looking mighty fired and disheartened. Then with Foster's guy leading the final set 5-2 and within moments of certain victory, I heard: "Now what do you want to settle for, Eddy?"

Sheepishly, the younger man offered, "Two-fifty."

"Not enough."

Finally they agreed on four hundred, and Eddy slid the appropriate chips across the table and the bet was canceled. After that the long-haired player sprang to life. He started lobbing perfectly over his opponent's head and smashing hot liners just inside the boundaries. Before you knew it, the match was over. Eddy's man won. Too bad the bet was already settled!

"Can't say I wasn't fair about it," Foster emphasized. "I let you choose who you wanted."

Eddy agreed, nodding dismally.

But I'm here to tell you, a man has to be careful in the treacherous world of gambling!

Sometimes when a guy gives you an even break, there's something unexpected lurking just out of sight.

As the announcer summarized the match, the camera zoomed in close on the departing tennis buffs. And there, still seated in the third row of the stands, was Foster, smiling.

47 Should Everyone Gamble?

A consistent winner usually has an even temperament. He doesn't get himself all boiled over worrying about occasional losses. Also, he doesn't skip and jump gleefully every time he makes a big score. Professional gamblers usually take both their losses and their wins in stride.

I don't normally give fatherly advice to near-strangers, but there was this one twenty-two year-old kid named Sammy who'd been showing up every week for a game near Corpus Christi. Away from the poker table, he was just as calm as could be, but get him a few thousand loser and he just turned hysterical.

Sammy isn't the only gambler I've known like that. I'd guess just about half of all gamblers have some emotional problems. They say that as the years wear on, the nicest players become really irritable. The ups and downs of professional poker can take their toll. On the other hand, some of the nastiest, most unpleasant players I grew up with mellowed out and became gentlemen over the years.

Poker is a strange occupation. You never know how it's going to bend your personality. But likely as not, it will bend it. Sammy had the worst case of bad poker manners you'll ever come across. He was a pretty astute poker player, and he had the ability to play a very competitive game. It's just that sooner or later his emotions always got the best of him and, as a result, he generally lost. Particularly, I remember this one night.

"Good to see you, Doyle. How's things going?" he greeted me pleasantly.

"Fine. You?"

"Oh, I'm fine, Doyle. Look, I wanna apologize for the way I acted last week. It wasn't you I was mad at when I flung them cards at you. Heck, you got as much a right to sandbag as anyone else. I'd a done the same to you if I had your hand."

He slapped me gently on the shoulders. I couldn't help but feel some warmth toward him, because this seemed to be his genuine personality and that monster he turned into every week at the poker game was something alien to him.

I said, "Don't worry about it, Sammy." And his eyes got almost misty—that's how emotional he was.

For the first few minutes of hold 'em, Sammy contained himself. Then he called all the way with a pair of sixes in the pocket and lost to two pair. He knew he shouldn't have done it, but instead of just scolding himself and quietly determining to gear down—the way most professionals would—he let it get him aggravated.

Even though he didn't play the next few hands, you could see him gnawing at his tongue and reliving the mistake again and again in his head. When he got an opportunity to play the next hand, he flung his chips in fitfully. This time he had the best hand, but he got drawn out on. He got up and kicked his chair, cursing.

Pretty soon he wasn't making any effort to win at all. Instead, he was playing practically every pot, throwing cards and whining. Although he didn't realize it, he had no chance of winning whatsoever. He kept excusing his play, complaining about his misfortune and jamming as many chips into the pot as he could.

Purely out of kindness, an older player suggested, "Hey,

kid, why don't you take a walk or something? Get some fresh air. Cool yourself down."

Sammy lurched up and swung wildly at the man, missing. Perhaps he had really intended to miss, I don't know. The host had to ask him politely to leave, and although we thought he would be permanently barred, somehow he had called up to apologize during the next week and had been invited again.

You'd think that, following that incident, Sammy would have held his behavior in check, even if it meant sitting on his hands to control his rage. But the very next week, he threw the cards so hard at a cowboy named Travis that they split the cigar he was smoking right down the middle. Lordy, this was just about the strangest sight I'd ever seen. There sat Travis, trying to suck on a cigar that had a jack and ace of diamonds smoldering right in the middle.

Everyone got real quiet real fast. I mean, Travis was mighty mean if he needed to be, and this looked like war. It was a long, crazy silence, and nobody wanted to butt in. The stage belonged to Travis and Sammy, and it was up to one of them to speak. Travis glared and glared while Sammy averted his eyes. Then, when Sammy finally did meet his gaze, Travis just spoke two words, dead serious: "Go home." Sammy cashed out and never returned to the game.

I bumped into him at another game in San Antonio a few months later. He was losing steady. His poker temperament had not improved. After one bad loss he approached me for advice. "Please, Doyle, I think I'm drowning. What am I doing wrong?"

"You're in the wrong profession, Sammy. You've got to quit."

"But I know this game as good as anyone!"

"I reckon you do, son. But you'll never win at it. It's hard enough facing a whole table of opponents, but you have to do that plus you have yourself to fight. That's too many against one. Give it up."

He seemed grateful and said he'd think about it. It was no use; he kept playing. He kept getting barred and he kept getting broke. I've always believed there are some folks in this world that just shouldn't gamble.

My years of action at the poker tables have taught me a lot about human nature. This book was written over twenty years ago and is still applicable. Games have changed and so have their players, but the theory remains the same. At a time when poker is more popular than ever, the messages in these anecdotes are sure to ring true.